Corporate Godfathers

The Career Management Handbook from Hell

Segreto Uno

CGW
PUBLISHING

2011

Corporate Godfathers

The Career Management Handbook from Hell

Segreto Uno

First Edition: November 2011

ISBN 978-1-9082931-1-4

© Segreto Uno 2010

'CGW' and 'CGW Publishing' are trading names of Revelation Consulting Limited. Registered in England and Wales, number 6984624. Registered office: Innovation House, South Church Enterprise Park, Bishop Auckland, Co Durham, DL14 6XB, United Kingdom.

Published by:

CGW Publishing
B 1502
PO Box 15113
Birmingham
B2 2NJ
United Kingdom
www.cgwpublishing.com

This life of ours, this is a wonderful life. If you can get through life like this and get away with it, hey, that's great.

But it's very, very unpredictable. There's so many ways you can screw it up. So you gotta think, ya gotta be patient. A lotta guys they're yanking their zipper before their dick's put away, then they wonder why they got snagged.

And they don't know when to zipper their fucking mouth shut, either.

Paul "Big Paulie" Castellano

Deceased Capo di tutti capi of the Gambino Family of New York

A Work of Fact or a Work of Fiction?

I wanted to get a reaction to this manuscript before submitting it for publication, so I asked a book reviewer who doesn't know me or anything about me to take a look at it. She read for about five minutes, and said: "This is scary. Is it a work of fiction?"

I answered, "How much truth can you handle?"

She caught her breath, picking up the implication of my question. A shadow of fear passed over her eyes.

I said, "If it makes it easier for you, just go ahead and call it fiction. You'll rest easier at night. But remember what Harry Truman said, "I never give them hell. I just tell the truth and they think it's hell."

Segreto Uno, 2010

Exposed: Blueprint for a Mob Takeover of American Business

What you are about to read is the most outrageous management takeover plan ever written - secret until now. Should you discover my real moniker somebody might knock on my door in the middle of the night and I'll answer to find a pair of thugs asking questions with their fists. Not an appealing scenario.

Here's the shocking truth: The Mob is infiltrating its bright, ambitious and loyal young men and women[1] into America's top corporations at entry level or middle management positions. The intent is to do whatever necessary to advance their careers until they're occupying the top positions of chairman of the board and chief executive officer. That's when the pillaging begins in earnest, when the mob controls the corporation and its cash flow, the lifeblood of any commercial business. And of course that's when it will be able to launder tons of illegal cash from criminal enterprises, the perfect cover. Its insidious plan assures The Mob a never-ending stream of cash flow and eye-popping profits.

Now here's where it departs from classic mob operations with a new and dangerous twist. The heads of major crime families put their heads together and created an affiliation, called The Association. It's composed of the leaders of the Italian Mafia (New York and New Jersey), Irish Mafia (Boston), Jewish Mafia (Miami, Chicago, Los Angeles) and the Russian Mafia (Brooklyn and Philadelphia). These powerful underground organizations have combined their talents and resources to fund and operate this daring plan.

Missing from The Association's roster are the Mexican Mafia and the Asian Mafia. This is because America's largest and most powerful companies are controlled largely by white men and a few white women, requiring white management recruits. No insult intended. Perhaps someday, as the American executive suite becomes more tolerant and open to other ethnicities, Black, Mexican and Asian gangsters can join The Association's effort to subvert Corporate America, too.

Put simply, The Association intends to take over American business. Not all of it, mind you, just enough to control the purse strings of the dominant corporations in every major American business sector. Companies in such diverse fields as investment banking, insurance, software and Internet commerce, TV broadcasting, publishing, movie studios, and consumer and industrial products manufacturing. The masterminds who devised the scheme and drafted the original plan of conquest have already implemented the first phase, so it's up and running. These wise old men, the heads of major crime, call their plan, with a tip of the hat to Paul Castellano, a departed capo di tutti capi, Corporate Godfathers.

It's going to take twenty - maybe thirty - years to complete the takeover. But leaders of The Association are patient. They predict illegal operations such as gambling, prostitution and drugs will eventually be taken over by legal businesses or governmental bodies resulting in The Mob's collapse. Therefore, Corporate Godfathers is The Mob's future. Or more correctly, The Association's future.

The Story of a Lifetime Falls into My Lap

Here's how I found out about The Association. While in New York for an appearance on a national TV show to discuss my latest book, I was eating lunch at a café when a broad-shouldered man dressed in casual wear covered by an open raincoat approached my table and asked to join me. I was taken aback (In NYC you never know what kind of nuts you're going to run into), but he looked sane and my curiosity got the better of me, so I nodded and he sat down.

He wore a baseball cap that covered part of his face, sunglasses that hid his eyes and a well-groomed beard that might have been false, but I couldn't tell. He identified himself as a member of a secret society but would not reveal the name of that society or his own name or any other identifying information. He said my reputation as a published writer and a former company president attracted him and he had a story to tell. Would I be interested? He had a cultured voice, spoke well, but occasionally slipped and revealed coarse language more reminiscent of the Jersey docks than Harvard Square.

How he knew of me is hard to say; he would not tell me other than to say he had read a few of my business books and articles. I have many contacts, several who might have mentioned my name. I also worked as president of an Italian-owned company in the USA, lived in Italy for a short period of time and knew "businessmen" whose backgrounds might be considered suspect in polite society.

I was wary about this intrusive stranger's story. Nevertheless, I asked him to continue. He told me that my work as a management writer greatly impressed his superiors, and they borrowed advice from my books on business and management to devise a handbook of their own[2]. While I was flattered, I of course was curious to know the organization he was referring to. I asked him its name. He glanced around, leaned forward and whispered the name of the secret society he belonged to: La Cosa Nostra. That floored me. It also scared the hell out of me. He was talking about the Mafia and I wasn't at all sure I wanted to hear anything more.

He reached across the table when I started to get up and pinned my wrist to the table. This frightened me even more. "You won't regret it," he said. "It's the story of the decade. Maybe the century." That got my attention. Somewhat reluctantly, I sat back down and listened while he outlined his story.

And what a story it was. I pushed lunch aside and spent an hour that day sipping coffee while Mr. X, as I called him, exposed The Association and its nefarious plan. He let me jot notes but nixed the digital recorder I always carry. Nor would he name companies and Association members. Just to make sure I wasn't carrying a wire he frisked me before we started talking in earnest. He told me enough to whet my appetite, and we made plans to meet again when he promised to reveal more juicy details. He extracted a promise from me to write the book exposing The Association. I tentatively agreed, still not convinced this was either the making of a colossal hoax or a true story that might place me in harm's way. When I tried to give him my cell phone number he smiled and said he knew it. That alone shook me. How much about me did he know? Apparently a lot. Still, I felt compelled to hear the end of the story (the Achilles heel of all writers).

Thankfully, I have a good memory and from the notes I transcribed during our initial meeting and the next two, both in Atlanta, where we met in Delta's Crown Room at the airport - Mr. X remaining incognito as during our first meeting, both times with slight but sufficient modifications in his disguise to alter his appearance, such as a mustache and goatee instead of the beard he wore the first time we met - I was able to reconstruct our conversations. At the second meeting, and the third, he showed me The Association's takeover plan but wouldn't allow me to take or run copies from it. Nor would he let me record his voice on my digital recorder. Instead he read most of it aloud or held the manual one page at a time in front of me while I scribbled furiously until my fingers cramped.

At the conclusion of our third meeting he made me promise to destroy my notes after I wrote the book. He was concerned that in the wrong hands his cohorts might be able to identify him. He had a point. At our first meeting I surreptitiously wrote a description of him and it didn't go unnoticed. He grabbed the paper from my hands and, visibly upset, ripped it up and threatened me[3]. I'm sure that act alone aroused his suspicions, and he was undoubtedly afraid some other identifying material might find its way into the finished manuscript. He said after I wrote the manuscript we would meet again one final time when he would proofread and edit what I had written. He wanted - demanded - that I hand over my handwritten notes to him at that final meeting. I swore I would but I never heard from him again. What happened to him, I'll never know, but nobody came knocking at my door in the middle of the night, so I'm reasonably confident The Association didn't learn about me from him. Assuming, of course, that The Association truly exists. I have no definitive proof of its existence and no way of investigating further. Nor do I really want to. My purpose here is to tell this astonishing story and disclose The Association's career management handbook.

Needless to say, my life has not been the same since. After our last meeting I hid the notes and kept them hidden for a couple of years until I worked up the nerve to take them out and write this book. All the time looking over my shoulder. I honored Mr. X's request and destroyed the notes after completing the manuscript. Not just for his sake, but for mine.

To return some calm into my life I put aside The Association connection and attempted to write the book in the form of management advice as proposed by nefarious corporate schemers, leaving out The Mob connection. I abandoned that effort when I realized, that despite my misgivings, I felt compelled to report the entire story, not just part of it. The sacred obligation of every writer.

Am I concerned for my safety? Of course I am but there's little of substantive value I can reveal about Mr. X or his role in The Association (if any). Nor if, in fact, there even is an Association. And, now that the book has been written and bought by a publisher I can no longer be considered a threat. Still, I frequently have sleepless nights; I keep a handgun by my side at all times and I have a permit to carry. If I had to do it all over again, would I? Yes, because I'm both a reporter and a book writer. That's what I do.

Why was Mr. X risking everything to expose this cunning scheme? Because, as he told me, he is a patriot who loves his country. His first allegiance is to the flag and he doesn't want to see it trampled in the dust. As he told me, that's what will happen to it if The Association gets its hooks into the country's top American corporations. From there it's not difficult to imagine The Association's foray into American politics. They know how to buy-off or threaten those who stand in their way, and they're not afraid of compromising key members of Congress and the White House, not to mention the federal courts. According to Mr. X The Association already "owns" certain municipal, county and state court judges, although he never mentioned names or places. It doesn't take an Einstein to understand the corrosive effect should The Association wield widespread political power.

What he said makes a certain kind of perverted sense. If you believe things are bad now, you ain't seen nothing yet! We'll morph into a country where five percent of the citizenry owns everything and ninety-five percent owns nothing and are virtual slaves to the top five percent - a heinous collection of gangsters, politicians and business chieftains with their greedy hands foraging in one another's pockets.

I sometimes wonder if The Association played a role in the 2008 collapse of both investment and commercial banking (Lehman, Countrywide, Bear Sterns, Merrill Lynch, etc). If you accept as fact that The Association has its people planted deep within the bowels of American business, it's not a stretch to believe some of the bankruptcies were the result of payoffs and money laundering practiced on a grand scale with sophisticated financial trickery. Perhaps we'll never know.

The Career Management Handbook from Hell

What you'll read on the following pages is the plan Mr. X described to me: how the mob intends to infiltrate and take over major American corporations. Obviously, when you're trying to read the scribbles I made from a handwritten career management handbook, and the writing is often indecipherable, you have to interpret and embellish somewhat. That I have done here, but it does not alter the essence of the story, nor its chilling intent.

This is a career management handbook from hell, designed for The Mob's best and the brightest; the young mobsters (called management recruits) The Association is using to infiltrate American business. The handbook was designed by The Association's first management recruit, a former Italian-American Mafia soldier who now holds a commanding position in a large and well-known but unnamed American consumer products company. The handbook he wrote, the one you'll read on the following pages in its entirety, describes lessons he learned from observing the dirty tricks applied by successful corporate managers on their rise to the peak of the corporate pyramid. And, of course, the dirty tricks he brought to the table himself, which were considerable. The handbook reads like a Machiavellian primer for corporate schemers, and that's essentially what it is. Consider it a blueprint describing what to do and what not to do to succeed in Corporate America at any expense. Exactly as The Mob is playing it. He's passing along this valuable information to The Association's management recruits, business neophytes really, who are venturing into unknown corporate waters for the first time in their careers.

Mr. X told me that three dozen or so young members recruited from the Italian Mafia, the Irish Mafia, the Russian Mafia and the Jewish Mafia are in their early stages of corporate training and indoctrination. This was over three years ago when we last met; imagine how many more Association recruits have infiltrated large corporations since. Corporate Godfathers is well underway and if something isn't done soon, it may be too late to stop The Association's evil plot to subvert the American way of life.

The career management handbook from hell, as you will see, is organized into sections, each covering subjects management recruits are obliged to master. Included are the ten management commandments for corporate success developed by The Association. Believe me, they are a far cry from the Bible's Ten Commandments.

At the end of each section, the author sums up the section's most compelling points. There are fifteen sections in all, every one of them chock full of deceptive strategies and tactics designed to advance the careers of The Association's management recruits.

If you work in Corporate America, look over your shoulder. The newcomer in your company may be an undercover gangster, a sworn Association blood member on the make. Whatever you do, don't cross that person. Not if you value your career... and possibly your life.

Read on and take care. From here on, everything you read is The Association's Career Management Handbook. Learn from it and pass it on. Hopefully it will scare you into doing something about it. Assuming enough ordinary citizens understand the consequences of The Association's scheme, it may not be too late to stop them.

The Association's Career Management Handbook

For Members Who Have Infiltrated America's Top Corporations.

Copies Assigned by Number and Tracked.

Restricted to Family Bosses, Underbosses, Consigliere and Designated Management Recruits.

Do NOT Otherwise Distribute.

Contents

SECTION ELEVEN

The Association's Seventh Management Commandment

SECTION TWELVE

The Association's Eighth Management Commandment

SECTION THIRTEEN

The Association's Ninth Management Commandment

SECTION FOURTEEN

The Association's Tenth Management Commandment

SECTION FIFTEEN

The Management Recruit's Code of Conduct

ENDNOTES

START HERE

Introduction and Instructions for Management Recruits

Instructions for reading this handbook and learning its lessons

The Future of the Association

You're about to find out what it takes to land a meaningful job and succeed in Corporate America. You'll also find stories of those who have failed and why they failed, as object lessons so you don't make the same mistakes.

Not that The Association expects you to fail. To the contrary, it expects you to succeed wildly - without exception. You are among the brightest of our combined organizations; you have been hand picked and undergone rigorous examination to assure that you are capable of achieving executive status in American business in a reasonably short period of time.

The Association has invested a lot of time and money in you. It has gained you entrance to some of the most exclusive colleges and universities this country has to offer, and supported you during your four years of study. All of you have graduated, or will graduate, from prestigious schools such as Princeton, Harvard and Yale. Need I remind you that The Association expended a lot of political capital to gain your college admittance and that your education cost a small fortune?

So let me emphasize up front, success is not only desirable, it's mandatory. The Association must realize a healthy return on you, its prime investment. Your job is to enter the business world and climb the corporate ladder until you've achieved executive status and are in control of your corporation's destiny. At that time The Association will issue further instructions.

Not that you'll be alone on your journey. The Association will be next to you every step of the way, providing the necessary coaching when you need it. But coaching is one thing, dependency is another; leaning on The Association to handle your problems is not desirable. So remember this when you're overwhelmed with problems that appear intractable - you are still on your own. The more you ask for help from home the greater the risk that Association leaders will consider you weak. You don't want that. Besides, your ability to resolve problems without help will strengthen you and give you the confidence to tackle additional responsibilities as you climb the corporate ladder.

This journey will take years. You can expect to spend the next twenty or thirty or forty years in Corporate America, remaining on the job as long as The Association deems necessary. You knew this when you agreed to undertake this assignment, so it will come as no surprise that you are making a lifetime commitment.

Until four years ago when you embarked on this project at the college selected for you, your entire work environment had been restricted to loan sharking, shakedowns, protection, gambling, drugs, hijackings, burglaries, murder and prostitution, so you are unfamiliar with the corporate world. You may not realize it but you come well equipped for your corporate journey. The basic difference between punching and kicking a deadbeat who has failed to pay his vig and outsmarting, out-tricking and out-flanking your job adversaries in corporate corridors is one of degree and method. You will find that corporate managers are just as vicious as you are, but more sneaky and not as overt or ready to use physical force. On the surface they're all smiles; behind the smiles lurk the most cunning and scheming minds you're likely to encounter anywhere. As you will see, in Corporate America sly and furtive qualities are in, demonstrations of anger and brutal direct action are out. Count on being attacked by clever adversaries as soon as you enter the corporate world at your modest level, and expect the attacks to continue and intensify as you move up the corporate ladder.

Consider this a how-to-manual in every sense of the phrase. You will learn how successful corporate executives figuratively cut the throats of their adversaries, steal their bosses' jobs and enhance their reputations through deceit and chicanery. These are your new role models. Learn well from them as I have from mine.

I went through the very same program you will experience but at an earlier stage. I was the guinea pig, or as I would now describe it in more educated terms, the pilot plant. Now I'm two steps away from the top position in my company. A very large consumer products company. So I know the ropes, and indeed, I wrote much of this career management handbook based on my experiences, supplemented by what I learned from shrewd corporate schemers.

I have taken a few liberties in writing the handbook. One of my talents is writing clear prose that is easy to understand. I enjoy telling stories. To that end I have sometimes constructed imaginary conversations for purposes of driving home different points through dialogue and narrative. While some of it may be imaginary, the points it emphasizes are real world.

Each section of the handbook is devoted to a specific subject. At the conclusion of each section you'll find a summary of the section's main points. Learn these well, for they constitute the essence of a successful corporate journey.

The future of The Association is in your hands. Although you may stumble on your pilgrimage to the top, you must not disappoint. There can be no excuses for failing to reach the pinnacle of your company. Failure, as they say, is not an option.

Don't hesitate to call on me if you need help. Use the cell phones reserved exclusively for that purpose; you will receive a new one every month. Destroy, not discard, the older cell phone. Whatever you do, do not allow your cell phone or assigned copy of this handbook to find its way into others' hands. Protect the handbook with your life, for it reveals our plans. And need I remind you, to paraphrase Big Paulie Castellano's advice regarding this thing of ours, "Keep your fucking mouth shut."

Good luck.

SECTION ONE

Shitcanned And Desperate: Anatomy of a Loser

Studying the mistakes corporate losers make:
Learning what not to do

I'm going to start by painting an ugly picture in words for you, a picture of how to lose at the great American game of business. You can learn a lot by studying corporate losers, so pay attention. After I've drawn this picture, I'll reach conclusions that will be instructive.

First, accept this fact: You know next to nothing about corporate life. Your work associations until now have been among fellow mobsters whose modus operandi has been, "Don't waste time taking names, just kick ass." Well, in Corporate America it seldom works that way. Those who make it to the top of the corporate pyramid are smoothies who mask their true feelings while deftly administering figurative knife thrusts to the kidneys of job adversaries. I'll explain as we go along.

Let's begin by talking about a guy named Charley I met in a sports bar one rainy Sunday during football season. He had been manager of customer service for a Silicon Valley dot.com company. Here's his sad story as I was able to piece it together (story and dialogue embellished for dramatic effect):

It happened Friday afternoon about 4:15 p.m., the way it usually does. Charley's boss, Pete, called him into his office. Pete was more harried than usual, had trouble meeting Charley's eyes, instead waved to a seat in front of his desk. Charley sat down and gripped the arms of the chair so tight the leather squeaked. Poor bastard's blood pressure always zoomed off the charts when the boss called him into his office.

Pete took a deep breath. "Look, Charley, let me tell you up front, you've been one hell of a good employee and a friend. You've worked for me five years now, and I've got nothing but good things to say about you. You know that."

Charley tensed, knowing when Pete heaped praise on one of his direct reports it was often a prelude to bad news. But he decided to play it straight: "That's exactly what you said in my annual performance reviews, Pete. All of them. And I'm grateful."

Pete winced. "Yeah, well . . ." His voice trailed off.

The tension Charley felt ratcheted up a few notches. Something's wrong, he told himself. Something bad.

"Look, there's no easy way to say this," Pete said, "so let me blurt it out." He took a deep breath and plunged ahead. "The company's under the gun. I don't have to tell you because of the market crash last year profits are down, way down, and sales for the past eighteen months have been an unmitigated disaster. To make a long story short, the brass has decided to do away with the entire customer service function here at home and ship it overseas to India."

Charley felt the blood drain from his face. "Does that mean the whole department's going to be laid off?"

Pete nodded.

"Me, too?"

"Unfortunately."

"My God," Charley replied, stunned. "I don't believe it. Customer Service has been a top performer. Never failed to meet budget. The customers love us. Hell, we even received a commendation from the chairman of the company for a job well done."

Pete leaned over his desk and frowned. He folded his hands and peered at them as if they were the most intriguing objects he had ever seen. "You're making it difficult for me, Charley."

"Well, pardon fucking me, it's just my job and livelihood. Not to mention all the people working for me."

"The layoff wasn't my idea."

"No, of course, not," Charley snarled, on the edge of losing control. "You had no part in this."

Pete replied in a strained voice. "Believe it or not, I didn't. The orders came directly from upstairs, unbeknownst to me."

"Ill bet you're not getting laid off."

Pete winced again. "No, I'm not."

"How much severance pay do we get?"

"There's a standard package for you and your employees. It's spelled out in the Procedures Hand—"

"I know what the Procedures Handbook says and the severance pay sucks. All of us with less than ten years service, and that's my entire department, including me, get a month's salary and insurance for three months. Then we're on our own."

"I'm sorry. What else can I say?"

Charley's world felt as if it were splintering into a thousand pieces. He didn't see the layoff coming and was floored. Worse, he was professionally and personally unprepared for this emergency.

Not only did Charley fail to pick-up the signs well in advance of the layoff, he also failed to position himself so he had options when the axe fell. A more astute player would have been ready with another job waiting in the wings. Not being prepared for the worst case scenario is unforgivable for a family man or woman who shoulders the responsibility of feeding and clothing the kids. Had Charley done his homework, Pete would have been passing the bad news to some other poor schlep, not him.

Charley screwed up big time.

You must never allow this to happen to you. Charley is a loser, and what you have read is the typical plight of a civilian[4] corporate manager, one not as motivated to succeed or as clever or as determined as you are. It's important to understand him, what his concerns are and why he failed. During your career you will encounter hundreds of Charleys, and you must learn not only how to handle them and use them to your benefit, but more important, how to avoid their fate. Let's examine others like Charley and see what lessons we can acquire.

The Psychology of Losers

Many like Charley (or his female equivalent, Charlene) are out of work or, if they're still clinging to the jobs they have, an unsettled feeling in the pit of their stomachs tells them it's soon coming to an end. Undoubtedly, it will. Just as quickly as their companies can arrange to ship their jobs to India or China, paying their replacements ten percent of what Charley or Charlene earns. Nobody's told them yet, but these corporate innocents have about three months to look for new jobs before they're unceremoniously kicked out.

It's bad enough without getting the axe. Their take-home pay sucks. Taxes, the mortgage payment, health insurance premiums and car payments make their paltry salaries disappear with discouraging regularity, with little left over for the basic necessities of life such as food, amenities and an occasional beer with friends after work on Friday night. (Man - or woman - does not live by bread alone.)

To make matters worse, their financial situations stink. Typical lower to middle management corporate employees have maybe three or four grand in savings, just about that much in company 401s and five hundred or a thousand bucks in checking accounts. All of which will vanish in a matter of months after they're shitcanned. And, of course, the government will tax the poor bastards for early withdrawal of their 401s.[5]

Most are married and most have children. Many of their spouses work as temps, bouncing from company to company, often on a weekly basis. They make minimum wage and have no health insurance. Their small paychecks go directly into the stomachs and on the backs of their growing kids in the form of food and clothes.

They work so hard that between the demands of job and home they're frizzled by day's end and drop off to sleep at 9:00 p.m. on the sofa watching boring reruns of Larry King. No sex for anybody, horny or no. They're cut-off.

The kids. Shit, the kids are always bitching. Their delicate palates require truffles and pâté de foie gras rather than the spaghetti and hot dogs that corporate wage slaves can barely afford to feed them. And they demand new soccer uniforms, gold school rings, clothes from the Gap and fashionable high-top sneakers that cost an obscene three-hundred bucks a pair.

Charley and Charlene feel frustrated by their inability to provide for their families, disheartened by their chances to get another decent job and desperate for an opportunity to somehow move ahead of the pack. They're almost out of work, out of money and out of hope. Not a pretty picture.

Literally millions of wage and salary earners share this predicament. Their smallish salaries vanish weekly with disquieting regularity as they pay the mortgage, car expenses, utilities and phone bills (a land-line plus four cell phones; hell, the kids must have their cell phones and text messaging. Only a cruel and heartless parent would deprive them of this necessity of life).

Now that you understand a little more about the typical corporate type you're likely to encounter throughout your career, let's see how you fit in the picture.

Not Everybody is Getting Shitcanned

When you get your new job in Corporate America and the promotions that follow, you must fight to protect them. Each and every job. Each and every time. Regardless of what level of the organization you find yourself. The combat only intensifies as you climb the corporate ladder. To forge ahead in business you'll need to employ tactics that other, more virtuous (and unwitting) employees would never consider. But given your background in organized crime, those tactics, or variants of them, should be as familiar to you as free doughnuts to cops. Minus the rough stuff, of course. You simply cannot beat the living shit out of your corporate adversaries using a set of brass knuckles. This adjustment from direct action to more subtle and underhanded techniques will be your biggest behavioral hurdle. Undoubtedly, you are accustomed to the more direct approach dealing with problems. My advice: Fugateaboutit!

Nevertheless, do not underestimate your adversaries. You will need to defend yourself against others intent on keeping their jobs at your expense. Adversaries who will do whatever it takes to protect their positions in the corporate structure, regardless of what they have to do or whom they have to do it to. Corporate managers routinely practice deception, guile, ruthlessness, deceit and chicanery; everything but physical force. All with a smile plastered on their game faces. These dirty players have an unfair advantage over you if you play by rules of acceptable corporate behavior. If they're willing to fight it out figuratively in the gutter and you're not . . . well, the end result of that game is clear. Those lacking the subtle cutthroat skills needed to handle the merciless demands of the early 21st century will soon find themselves slipping off the corporate ladder, and often as not out the corporate door, rudely shoved aside by tougher, more hardened competitors. Need I mention that your fate is tied to your corporate success? Failure, as I've mentioned before, is not an option.

The typical corporate loser has probably tried everything else to hold onto his job, the whole Horatio Alger routine: working long hours; offering lots of suggestions to improve quality and productivity without taking credit; showing loyalty to the boss and the company; displaying a willingness to help other employees; dedicating themselves to the job above family. Oh yeah, they've trod the worn grooves of that path, just like zillions of others before them.

And what has it got them? Zero, nada, niente, nothing, zilch. Not when their companies can cut costs by letting thousands like them go.

On their last day at work, the more hapless among them, clutching pink slips in hand, look around and notice that some employees are still working, even flourishing in hard times. They ask why. Why am I fucked by the fickle finger of fate, and not the other guy or gal?

In Corporate America the longevity of survivors rarely has anything to do with seniority. Lots of unemployed men and women with high company seniority wait on line at the local church for a food handout while their less senior and less experienced brethren continue drawing paychecks. Lots of employees holding onto their jobs aren't necessarily the ones who worked the long hours or were the most creative or productive or put job over family. What gives them such an edge that even in hard times they always manage to survive?

You're about to find out. The techniques described on the following pages work. Upright citizens will label them sneaky, deceptive, even vicious, but those who criticize have jobs, full bellies and money left over to pay their kid's orthodontists. Most important of all: they do not have your imperative to succeed or perish trying.

This handbook will open your eyes to the reality of today's job marketplace, where for every well-paying job there are thousands of hungry applicants. Where for every promotion to a higher level of the company there are dozens, sometimes hundreds, of competitors. This handbook will assure that you start out with secure footing on the corporate ladder and continue climbing until you've achieved your ultimate success in the executive suite.

If the cutthroat world of business today is any indication, the future promises to be a doozy. As my old Uncle Anastasio[6] was fond of saying in his down-home Sicilian manner, "In such an environment, only the toughest, dirtiest and most realistic will survive and prosper. The rest are goose eggs for the fox."

Strategies from Section One[7]

1. You have no true friends where you work, only adversaries and business associates. So-called friends at work make you vulnerable. They know you well enough to understand your weaknesses and exploit them. Don't take a chance. Keep fellow employees at arm's length. Revealing too much could cost you a promotion, even your job. Confide in nobody at work. In the example at the start of Section One, Charley made the unpardonable error of thinking that Pete, his boss and "friend," would protect him from losing his job. Pete saved his own skin instead. That's human nature, and it's no different here than in organized crime. In fact, while organized crime protects its own, corporations and the executives who run them have no loyalty whatsoever to anything other than the bottom line. In such an environment employees are truly expendable.

2. There are untold numbers of employees and job candidates hungry to take your job away from you any way they can, especially in today's hostile business climate where good jobs are scarce and becoming scarcer. Keep that in mind and you'll stay alert, ready to combat any threat to your position. To think your job is secure is sheer folly. Your job is never secure, no matter what position you hold. There's always somebody in the wings, ready and eager to do whatever it takes, no matter how deceptive, to snatch your job. You must be more focused and more deceitful than your adversaries to survive.

3. Look upon your job as a general looks upon the battlefield. He is willing to make any sacrifice (anybody and everybody that is, except himself) to achieve his objective, no matter how terrible the price. The bloodier it gets the more frightened his enemies (ambitious peers) become. Few have the stomach or balls to challenge an adversary willing to "go to the mat" to keep his job. Make your plans and execute them ruthlessly and with vigor. Never look back, no matter the number of torn bodies scattered across the battlefield. Hesitate or feel pangs of remorse and you'll lose the battle (your job) and probably the war (your career . . . or worse).

4. Don't make the mistake of thinking, as Charley did, that a solid job performance alone will protect you. Sure, it's important, but it's not enough to save your skin. Politics always plays a role. Connected people survive while others flounder even when their job performance stinks. I'll explain how to get connected with the right corporate executives in the next section.

5. Plan a fallback position in case of a corporate shakeup. This means thinking two or more steps ahead on the corporate chessboard. Indeed, The Association encourages you to play the game of chess so you can assimilate the skill of forward planning. If you think of work as a game and you as a chess piece, that will give you the proper perspective to advance in Corporate America.

SECTION TWO

An Admittedly Common Thug Morphs into a Suave Prince of Business

How the author became the first of The Mob's plants in American business, and some basic lessons he learned along the way

Allow me, the author of this manual, to introduce myself. My name is Vito "College Boy" Ostinato[8]. If you speak Italian, you know the word "Ostinato" means tough. And tough I am. My former Mob associates nicknamed me "College Boy" because I'm the only one among them who attended college. Hell, I'm the only one of them who graduated from high school. Our work doesn't require much in the way of formal education. If you get what I mean.

You've already noticed I don't talk like a common fucking thug, but that's exactly what I am. Four years at Princeton and a Harvard MBA gave me the ability to speak like Barack Obama, but I'm a mobster, pure and simple. Always have been, always will be. And unashamed of it. My uncle is the capo di tutti capi of one of the local families: the big cheese, the Godfather; my father his consigliere, his chief advisor.

I was reared to become a mobster. At twelve years old I ran numbers after school for the neighborhood soldier. In high school I was a courier for the Family, carrying piles of cash across the country most weekends. Cash to payoff politicians. Cash for banks to launder. Cash to pay for hits. Dangerous work, but I never once failed to deliver the money on time and into the right hands.

The Family sent me to college to major in business and finance for a purpose. My father, along with the head of the Family, hatched this truly ingenious plan to insert me into a large, major corporation, one whose name you would immediately recognize but for obvious reasons will remain unidentified, and help me move up the ladder as swiftly as possible (using every ploy in the Family's grab bag of dirty tricks). Thereby placing me in a commanding position when the time came for the Family to take over the company.

A daring plan, one unique in concept, designed to move the Family away from "hot" businesses such as drugs (which eventually will be legalized, thereby depriving the Family of one of its prime revenue streams), and into a large legitimate business where cash flow is bountiful, allowing for frequent and hefty "withdrawals".

To that end, we formed an alliance with prominent Irish, Jewish and Russian "families" to work this scheme on a grand scale. As you know, we now call our august group The Association.

The Association's strategy involves infiltrating a few dozen key businesses over the next twenty to thirty years, and we're not talking mom and pop stores here. We're aiming at America's top companies. Can you imagine the impact on our profit and loss statement when The Association takes over management of the country's largest Wall Street firms, software and Internet commerce houses, publishing companies, movie studios, major TV networks and consumer and industrial products manufacturing companies? It's all a matter of bringing along the right soldiers as we Italians call them, those in The Association young enough and bright enough and ambitious enough to do what I have done. I'm talking about you. Consider me the template. The Association has great plans for American business. And what I have accomplished, you can, too.

Getting back to me: After ten years, I'm now the company's chief operating officer (COO) for - let's call it (not its real name, of course) - International MacroSystems, Inc., a high tech consumer products corporation employing 50,000 people. I'm one step away from the top executive post: CEO and Chairman of the Board. The top guy better watch his step. I'm after his job and I know how to get it. And get it I will.

My days as a mole will soon pay-off big time. I'll run one of the industry's most profitable corporations and yeah, you guessed it, populate the top executive ranks with men and women I can count on to be loyal to The Association. Code words meaning that while we may never own the majority of the company's common stock, or even a significant percentage of it, we will still own the company heart and soul. And nobody - I mean nobody - will dare defy us. Board members, shareholders, executives, suppliers, the Feds, nofuckingbody. Not if they know what's good for them.

I've Got an Offer You Can't Refuse

That brings me to this career management handbook. My intention is to let you know how successful corporate managers like me make it to the top: the strategies, tactics, techniques and methods we use on our journey to the executive suite. Valuable information you can apply to secure a job and earn promotions.

Let's plunge right in. Here's lesson number one: Assuming you're safely established in your company, you've got to recognize the signs of trouble, corporate style.

I say corporate style deliberately. At home you had no difficulty understanding where you stood. Fuck up and you were liable to get a clip alongside your head with the admonishment to straighten up and fly right. Blatant, direct stuff like that. In corporations it's much different, often so subtle you may not even be aware of criticism . . . until a year or two later when every one of your adversaries has been promoted and you find yourself stuck at your current management level. Then you'll realize that somewhere, somehow you fucked-up and now you're the corporate equivalent of road kill.

I could recite the usual litany of signs to watch for when you're number is up in Corporate America: your peers and boss start avoiding you; the boss ignores you when he passes you in the hallway and he won't look you in the eyes; your annual performance review is wishy-washy, neither good nor bad; even more telling, you don't get any performance review; you're no longer invited to meetings. Obvious hints like that.

By then it's too late. The die, as they say, is cast, and your fate is now in the hands of bosses who consider you and others like you disposable. That fate might be okay for a rabbit desperately burrowing into a hole, attempting to escape the fox, but not for you, not if you want to continue living and breathing and succeeding in Corporate America. There is a better way.

First, and most important, find a rabbi. No, not the religious kind. A special kind of rabbi. As practiced in the New York City Police Department, a rabbi is defined as somebody high up in the organization who looks out for you. Once you've located your target rabbi, do whatever it takes to cultivate him, and I mean whatever it takes. Your career may hang in the balance. Shine his shoes, deliver his morning Starbucks, flatter the ugly bastard. Pay a stripper to give him a blowjob. Anything to get his attention.

Case in point: When I started at International MacroSystems as a lowly financial analyst, I nosed around and became familiar with the top executives of the company. Unobtrusively, of course, and being careful not to make it apparent I was seeking a connection with somebody in the executive suite. That would have labeled me an ass kisser, a reputation nobody wants (although, if people are honest about it, damn near everybody drops their pants and squats when the boss yells shit). In any case, I wanted my peers and bosses to feel comfortable around me and let down their guards. Being known as an ass kisser defeats that purpose; it erects artificial barriers.

I found what I was looking for in Patricia Goodwelt, vice president of human resources, a forty-eight year old divorcée and career woman. Smart, tough, cold-hearted and believe me when I say it was difficult getting next to her, suspicious as she was of human nature. (The quintessential corporate human resources professional: somebody who both distrusts and dislikes people.)

I arranged to make enough trips to her office on personnel matters until finally meeting the lady. After I penetrated her reserve (put your dirty mind to rest. It's not what you're thinking; not yet anyway), I discovered she owned a purebred poodle she showed at dog shows across the country. Of course, I seized on that point, bullshitted my away around it to convince her I was also a dog show devotee. Needless to say, that evening after work I rushed to Barnes & Noble and bought a book on dog shows, read it cover to cover. Then managed to find my way to one of those shows and, surprise, run into, well, you guessed it: Patricia Goodwelt. What an amazing coincidence!

I applied my considerable charm wooing the lady. It wasn't long afterward we were playing hide the social sausage every Wednesday night at her exclusive park-front condo. I fit her needs: a handsome young guy, well-hung, hard body with a lot of sexual staying power. She fit my needs: a rabbi in high places and a good piece of ass as an added benefit. A perfect match, defined as me getting what I wanted from the arrangement.

Eventually, the grapevine had it that Patricia and I were, if you'll excuse the expression, cohabiting. That knowledge actually worked in my favor, making my adversaries wary of crossing me, afraid of retribution from a competitor with friends in high places.

Within months, the relationship with Patricia saved my ass. She tipped me off to an impending sale of my division. Even arranged for me to get a transfer into a high profile division of our company where she knew my skills would shine.

By the time Patricia left the company five years later, I was already well on the way to the top of the corporate pyramid, thanks in large part to her mentoring and running interference for me. Frankly, it was time for her to go. The sex between us had become well, routine.

Besides, I had made a more powerful ally, the chairman of the board.

Dare I mention that I keep in touch with Patricia? The lady became senior vice president of human resources for a major competitor, and who knows how she might once again serve my interests. Our paths cross every year or so at trade shows, at which time to keep our relationship alive we - if you'll once again excuse the expression - cohabit.

Incidentally, the same benefits I enjoyed with my rabbi hold true for Association women on the make. As all of us smart guys realize, it's easier for a woman to attract a man than the other way around. So ladies, be my guest. Use your womanly skills - as if you hadn't thought about it already, you sly devil. Go find your rabbi and drop your drawers.

The relationship of rabbi to mentor doesn't have to be sexual, but it does have to be close. You may form an ongoing association with your rabbi based on a common interest such as one where you both workout at the same gym. Or the rabbi may have lost a daughter and you find out about it and become his surrogate daughter. There are many, many such avenues to explore. A test of your ingenuity and competency will be to select the right rabbi and use the right approach to hook the sucker.

The Lifeblood of a Spy

Talk with any intelligence agent for any amount of time and you'll soon understand the importance of information. She'll tell you that information is king, inside information a kingdom. It's the lifeblood of a spy. With the proper information a spy can penetrate any organization and flourish. Lack of it lowers the probability of mission success and may even compromise the spy's safety.

Although you're not a spy, at least in the strict sense of the word, you need inside information to survive and prosper. What would have happened to my career at International MacroSystems had darling Patricia not informed me that my division was going to be sold? Chances are I would have been part of the sale, maybe even laid off. That would have meant failure, and failure in the eyes of The Association is unforgiveable. Inside information saved the day.

Remember when you were a kid and you played all those wonderful imaginative games with your toys or dolls, pretending you were a doctor or fireman or cop? Remember how engrossed you were and how much fun it was? Do the same now. Pretend you're a spy, uncover your future rabbi and devise a plan to get that rabbi rooting for you. Ferret out information from him to advance your career. A spy's viewpoint gives you the appropriate perspective to uncover information to help you avoid pitfalls and take advantage of blossoming opportunities. Treating it like a game makes it more enjoyable and less of an onerous task. Since you've got twenty or thirty years ahead of you in the corporate game, the more interesting you make the journey, the more satisfaction you'll derive from it.

Speaking of blossoming opportunities, when I moved up to middle management at International MacroSystems, an associate at a smaller competitor tipped me off that his company was getting out of the software games business and was considering a sale to one of my company's competitors. At the time I learned of the potential sale it was not yet public knowledge. A perfect example of juicy insider information waiting to be used. I knew my company was looking for an opportunity to enter the software games business. Question was how to use the information and with whom. I sure as hell wasn't about to share this delectable tidbit with just anybody.

So one day I "managed" to cross paths with the chairman of the board of my company in the company dining room during afternoon break. (My goodness, how coincidental and fortunate that meeting was, if you'll excuse my rampant cynicism. Of course, having studied the old boy's movements, I knew he liked to sip a cup of tea and skim the Wall Street Journal in the dining room every day about 3:00 p.m. Helped the poor overworked soul relax.) Needless to say, I passed along information of the potential sale to the chairman and volunteered to act as informal liaison, using my contact at the competitor, should the big boss be interested. He was immediately taken with the idea. We enjoyed a nice long chat while other executives in the dining room cast suspicious and envious glances in my direction. I had hit a home run first time at bat with the old boy. Not long afterward I was chairing a task force to look into acquiring the company. That meeting zoomed me ahead of my job competitors.

By "accidentally" running across the chairman, I avoided the criticism of going over my boss' head. Besides, why let my boss take credit for information I uncovered? After all, I was already taking credit for his contributions and damned if I'd let him turn the tables on me.

Within six months our company bought out the software games business and, need I say, I gained yet another champion in my company, this one at the highest possible level.

Oh yeah, I almost forgot. I got my boss' job.

Strategies from Section Two

1. Forget the tough guy persona you're accustomed to; it'll get you nowhere in Corporate America. Learn how to kiss ass without looking as if you're kissing ass. It's an art form and essentially a matter of nuance. You can emulate the herd and paste a phony smile across your kisser and drool at the mouth when you're sucking up to the boss, or you can be more discriminating and provide him with useful information that will make you stand out. Get the difference? All it takes is a little practice (and puckered lips).

2. Find somebody high in the organization who will take you under his wing and move you through the ranks at mach speed. Conduct your search both systematically and discreetly. First select somebody powerful, for example the president of your company, then find what trips his trigger (like the software acquisition just described with the chairman or the dog show with sweet Patricia Goodwelt), decide how and where you're going to approach him, then make your move. Without appearing as if it was orchestrated, which of course it will be. Cultivate him. One favor may not be enough to keep his attention. Don't forget his birthday and other important anniversary dates. And don't stop bringing him tidbits of information he can use. Make yourself indispensible. He may decide to use you as an information source, knowing full well that his direct reports are so busy kissing his ass and filtering information from him, he doesn't really know what's

happening on the firing line of the company. Oblige him; make him happy. Provide the information he desires . . . slanted in your favor, of course. But remember: it's a quid pro quo arrangement. He needs to get something valuable from it, too. Otherwise, the relationship will fizzle.

3. Which brings up the next principle. Information is key to corporate survival and success. To repeat myself, information is king, inside information a kingdom. Get it any way necessary: pay for it, bribe somebody for it or blackmail somebody for it (carefully so you don't get caught), listen covertly to conversations for it, pump the grapevine for it. But get it. Reward your subordinates as well as employees in other organizations within the company when they bring you inside information. Make them part of your team, your inner circle. Employees will always follow a winner. Just don't revert to the mob way of getting information by pummeling somebody with a baseball bat.

4. Dig out the dirt, particularly dirt that weakens your peers. When the crucial time comes, such as a promotion, and the boss has to select between you and a peer, drop a word or two on the grapevine about the time your peer was arrested on a peeping tom charge. But don't get caught spilling the beans. That's the kiss of death.

SECTION THREE

Like Shit Through a Screen

What HR looks for in an interview is worlds
apart from what your future boss wants.

You're not always going to have the advantage of Association connections to find an appropriate corporate job. Since The Association is a secret organization, its existence unknown to American business until now, you may be required to navigate the hiring process on your own. The purpose of this section is to show you how to do it successfully.

Hiring into Corporate America may be difficult given your background in organized crime, where entry to your respective family involved knocking heads, making a few hits and bringing in hoards of cash gained through illegal means (although, truth be told, nobody is more adept at bringing in hoards of cash gained through shady or illegal means than businessmen and Wall Street financiers). Needless to say, the art of interviewing for a corporate job is at the other end of the persuasion spectrum where truthfulness reigns - at least the appearance of truthfulness.

You can approach job interviews one of two ways. Being honest and forthright like the average job seeker, or devious and calculating like a true corporate schemer. Guess which approach locks up the job and which provides at best a fifty-fifty chance? I call this section "Like Shit Through a Screen" because if you can dish out the shit well enough, you can successfully pass through any human resources screen like, well, shit through a screen.

You should have no trouble lying, embellishing or stretching the truth and bullshitting your way through interviews convincingly once you absorb the techniques, because you already understand the art of persuasion; it's inherent in being a mobster. The Association selected you in part because of your ability to go beyond the usual head-knocking and engage with other people intelligently. In plain talk, the ability to sling the shit and convince people that your way is the right way. In our opinion a necessary aptitude for an Association member or anybody else for that matter, ascending the corporate ladder.

Here's an example. During my tenure at National MacroSystems I interviewed many job applicants. One stands out above all others. At the time I was director of sales and marketing. We were hiring for an important copywriter job in our high-visibility advertising department. The name this job candidate used on his resume was Harrison Bane Kennedy[9], a real WASP-sounding moniker. During the interview Harrison was articulate, presentable, bright, focused - and phony. I sensed it immediately after listening to him talk. He was, in fact, too glib, too polished, too over-the-top confident. And since it takes a crook (or a cop) to smell out another crook, I dug into his background.

Harrison Kennedy's real name turned out to be Mike Jankelowicz, a Polish sausage with pretensions from Chicago. He had no college degree, so upon discharge from the Marine Corps after eight years as an enlisted man, Mike shopped around the alumni databases of Ivy League schools until he found someone his age from Chicago with a degree in business. Working online he uncovered exactly the person he was looking for in one Harrison Bane Kennedy who graduated cum laude from

Harvard the same year Mike Jankelowicz was discharged from the Marine Corps. Harvard is a choice school that opens all sorts of doors. A made-to-order scam for a budding scam artist.

Now listen to how clever this guy was. He officially changed his name to Harrison Bane Kennedy, in effect stealing the real Kennedy's identity, at least for purposes of claiming a sheepskin from arguably the most prestigious college in America. He shaved four years off his military service, and alleged he spent that time attending Harvard. He even went so far as to visit the campus to learn his way around should somebody ask about Harvard.

Did I kick him out when I discovered the fake degree? Hell no. I figured somebody with that large a set of balls and the imagination to change his name to fake a degree would make substantial contributions if I channeled his efforts in the right direction. There's no alliance a crook likes better than one with another crook. Particularly a crook who owes you.

I let Mike know I was on to his game and watched his face blanch. When I told him I'd let him get away with his deception provided he busted his ass working for me, you'd have thought I'd handed him a reprieve from a death sentence. I instructed Mike to revise his resume and resubmit it without the fake degree. Of course, I kept a copy of the original phony resume, just in case Mike forgot who saved his ass. After that he was mine, body and soul. I owned Mike and the son-of-a-bitch knew it. Bottom line: The guy became a star performer. His bet paid off. And so did mine.

The Fannullones Obstacle

Harrison Bane Kennedy didn't fool me but he clearly fooled Human Resources (HR), the professionals responsible for screening out phonies and pretenders before they reach the next stage of the interviewing process. In my experience I have found some HR folks to be uninterested in their work, unimaginative and just plain lazy. In the Family we call such people fannullones, (literally "a do nothing." A pejorative Italian word that expresses the views of some that HR is often a repository of deadbeats and losers who failed at other jobs in the company). Such losers are also called il buffones (guess how that translates).

Now, don't get me wrong. Not all HR specialists are fannullones or buffones. Many are sharp and intuitive. The worst assumption you can make is that all of them are the kind of fannullones Harrison Kennedy fooled. If you assume that (remember the old saying, assume makes an ass out of u and me?), you're probably going to flunk the HR interview because you're either arrogant or dull-witted. If either of those derogatory adjectives describes you, get your face out of my handbook now! You're going nowhere, except back to where you came from to hustle enough cash to reimburse The Association for the money it wasted on your college education. Your future is uncertain . . . if you even have one.

The job candidates who successfully permeate the HR screen are those who understand that the purpose of Human Resources is to screen out job candidates, not screen them in. That's because of the staggering number of resumes and applications HR receives for any given job opening, particularly in our depressed economy. By necessity, HR will deliberately try to find something wrong with job candidates to whittle down the candidate pool, so that at the end of the interviewing funnel, HR is left with a handful of viable job candidates from the hundreds or thousands[10] they started with. Unfortunately, in its haste to narrow the field, HR too often sloughs off the best potential employees, which, God forbid, might include a job candidate from The Association.

For an astute job candidate such as you that means leaving nothing to chance. It means knowing ahead of time what characteristics and experience HR requires, and just as important, what characteristics and experience rule you out. But beware! Those same characteristics that HR favors may not dovetail with what the hiring manager[11] seeks. In fact, they rarely do, since HR comes at the screening process with a different set of expectations.

Because most hiring managers understand that breaking the mold leads to significant job improvements, they frequently expect new hires to be daring and unconventional in pursuit of company goals. Conversely, HR screens out such job candidates. Instead, it measures and approves job candidates on their ability to play it safe and follow the rules and not make waves. Exactly opposite of what the hiring manager seeks. HR stresses conformance over conflict, team playing over individual performance, structure over instinct, plodding efforts over imagination, Mr. Nice Guy over Mr. Bad Ass.

The quick-witted job candidate must know the requirements of both HR and the hiring manager before he steps foot in the company lobby, or be intuitive enough to ferret them out early in the interviewing process and prepare the "right" answers. He must similarly anticipate questions HR will have about negatives in his background that might rule him out, and have prepared answers for each. Negatives (as perceived by HR) such as job hopping, low salary, getting fired from a job or being unemployed for several months or longer. All of them serious disqualifiers.

You have a special problem. Most, if not all, of your experience will have been gained as a junior-level mobster. Obviously you cannot declare that background on your resume, but must have a fabricated background that will pass muster during the corporate interviewing process. To that end, The Association's corporate hiring expert will help you devise an "airtight" resume that will stand up to the highest scrutiny, including reference checks. Since this will be a different experience for you, she will also help you prepare through mock interviews for the real thing. She'll capture your performance on camera and critique it and repeat the process as often as needed until you can answer all anticipated questions and you feel comfortable in the interview setting. The following story will demonstrate the type of "background adjustments" you may need just to get your foot in the door.

Stanley Quick[12], a sharp guy I knew (non-Association) who understood the rules of the game, had a background in manufacturing management. His company folded and Stanley found himself on the street looking for a job in 2010 at a time when manufacturing jobs were as scarce as bank loans. He was forced into taking a series of low-paying jobs in construction, restaurant management and mall supervision to support his family. Finally, a recruiter found an opening for Stanley as manufacturing manager in a small, but well-heeled, plastic architectural products manufacturing company about fifteen miles from where Stanley lived. So far so good.

But the problem was how to handle the series of minor jobs on Stan's resume. While perfectly understandable to somebody hard-nosed like a manufacturing vice president, Stanley knew it would raise a red flag in HR, and he might never pass through its screen. He had to find a way around it.

Here's what he did. First, he prepared a functional resume that listed all of his strengths and accomplishments, but without listing employers or employment dates. This type of resume, as opposed to a chronological resume listing former jobs along with employment dates, is great for minimizing negatives. (It is beyond the purview of this career management handbook to examine in detail what a functional resume contains. You can either use The Association's hiring expert or find out for yourself by reading any number of books on the subject, or researching the subject online.)

For face-to-face interviews he decided to roll the series of minor jobs into a fictitious position as a consulting associate for a small family-owned management consulting firm he once worked for. The firm was still owned and run by a former boss whom Stanley had cultivated and kept in touch with over the years. As it turned out, wisely so. When Stanley explained the problem to his former boss, he was met with a sympathetic ear. The former boss, knowing the good work Stanley did for him, agreed to say that Stanley had worked as a contractor[13] for the period of time in question should HR call him. That addressed Stanley's problem and he sailed through the HR interview.

Was Stanley's former boss at risk? Most likely, provided he put his lie in writing. But he was smart enough not to do so, and he knew, based on Stanley's work record as a consultant, that Stanley would perform well on his new job and the issue would never arise. Neither was Stanley's resume fabricated since he used the functional resume format.

Stanley and his former boss were aware that their state had no laws prohibiting lying on resumes (some states do), and that Stanley's new employer had no contracts with the government, where lying on resumes could be considered an illegal act.

Stanley was a success as manufacturing manager for his new company, as his former boss knew he would be. He was later promoted to vice president of manufacturing and awarded a seat on the board of directors.

Since the hiring expert at The Association prepared your resume, she will have prepped every employment source, real or imagined, ahead of time to assure validation in case of reference checks. Nevertheless, it behooves you to double check your references since Murphy's Law (if anything can go wrong it will go wrong) is constantly in play. Your resume, regardless of who prepares it, and regardless of what's factual and what's contrived, is ultimately your responsibility. So do not casually flip off the necessity to prepare thoroughly for interviews. There's too much at stake for both you and The Association. The Association's hiring expert is there for support and help only, but the final resume and your use of it in job interviews is up to you.

As a further example of resourcefulness, one of our outstanding woman management recruits snookered the human resources manager during an employment interview and knocked out her competition. In her own words:

"A couple of years before The Association recruited me, I was vying for the job of cost accounting manager and preparing for my second interview. During a conversation with the headhunter I discovered that the company had narrowed the selection for the position to another candidate, a man, and me.

"I needed the job desperately. I'm a single mother with two young children and I had been on the street for six months, the result of a massive layoff by my previous employer. The guy I was competing against had more experience than me, most of it working as an accounting manager for a smaller firm. Stiff competition. It scared me silly.

"I figured the other guy would edge me out based on his managerial experience alone, and I had to do something to neutralize his advantage. So, I hatched a cagey scheme designed to level the playing field.

"I asked a women friend to call the HR manager and claim to be my job competitor's girlfriend. Not wife, girlfriend. She raised hell, telling the HR manager that the bastard got her pregnant and abandoned her. She was going to sue for child support and wanted the prospective company to garnish his wages.

"Well, no HR manager wants to handle a beef like that. It's got lawsuit and bad company publicity written all over it. Human Resources is so averse to anything controversial it will inevitably steer clear of job candidates with such problems, and understandably so. The phone call shook the HR guy up so much he never once questioned the veracity of the lady's story. The bottom line is that HR froze out my competitor and I got the job.

"Did I have sleepless nights because of this underhanded tactic? Frankly, no. Maybe I should have, but I quickly dispelled any possible feelings of guilt when I tucked my kids in at night in their comfortable beds in their comfortable home. I did what I had to do to provide for myself and my family and that's all there is to it."

Don't you know that this lady is going to be an outstanding management recruit?

As you are undoubtedly aware, members of The Association, in their former incarnations as separate mob families, did not employ women. That situation is no longer tolerable; not in a day and age when women are occupying the top jobs in many large companies. That imbalance called for a nationwide recruiting campaign to find exactly the right type of women for our program: women who are rapacious, determined to succeed, motivated by loyalty to The Association and the desire to make tons of money; women who are ball busters and know how to cut an opponent, man or woman, down to size, and love doing it. The campaign to locate such women was difficult but rewarding. We managed to enlist a handful of compelling women and our recruiting efforts continue to this day.

Women bring subtlety to the table, a trait often lacking in men who bring sledgehammers. And subtlety is what often spells the difference between success and failure in Corporate America, so women are a welcome addition.

Strategies from Section Three

1. The expectations of Human Resources are predictably so far removed from reality that during interviews you have no other choice but to find ways to neutralize your background negatives, even trivial ones. This means offering answers, real or imagined, that will satisfy the purist HR mind. Such dissemblance takes careful planning, and its seriousness should not be minimized.

2. The purpose of Human Resources is to screen out job candidates, not screen them in. When resumes for an advertised job start flowing in, HR immediately sorts them into two piles. The biggest pile contains resumes with perceived negatives. The second, much slimmer, pile contains resumes of those few who have no known negatives. HR will later assiduously examine the background of the second group to surface more potential disqualifiers. The search for negatives continues throughout the HR interviewing process until the list is whittled down and a few "clean" job candidates emerge. While those candidates might be squeaky clean they may not be the strongest for the job opening. So keep this in mind before sending out your resume: Make it as "clean" as possible, even when you have to conceal or camouflage negatives. You can do this by writing a functional resume, then applying your interview skills, using what you have learned here, to pass the HR screen. The Association's hiring expert, experienced in all matters HR, will help you write a resume HR fannullones will love.

3. Be prepared to complete a company job application where you're required to list the companies you worked for along with employment dates. Our hiring expert will help you devise an airtight resume and avoid the shortcomings that could rule you out of contention for the job opening. Remember the example of Stanley Quick.

4. There are a multitude of ways to talk around negatives such as a lack of proper education, job hopping, low salary, being out of work for several months, little experience or anything else that might surface in the HR fannullone's never-ending quest to screen out job candidates. Do what you have to do to stay in the game and sound convincing. But make your story persuasive and your resume airtight.

5. If you're on the other side of the hiring spectrum, it's always to your advantage to hire people who owe you, people you have something on, like Harrison Bane Kennedy in the example I described earlier in this section. Subordinates such as Harrison are motivated to go balls out in pursuit of your goals.

6. Above all, keep this in mind: No matter how cordial the HR interviewer is, he isn't your friend. Consider him your adversary and do whatever it takes to beat him at his own game. No tactic is too extreme. Whatever you do, and I know you're going to use your God-given ingenuity to pass through the screen, cover it with smiles and low key responses. Remember, HR does not favor strong personalities.

SECTION FOUR

Beating The Good Players at
Their Own Game

How to pass personality tests and ace in-depth
interviews with a clinical psychologist through
deceptive answers

The advent of personality testing in Corporate America was a wet dream for HR fannullones, since it gave them yet another way to rule out job candidates. Ostensibly it was designed as a tool to separate so-called "normal" people from compulsive failures, troublemakers and outright psychos. Instead personality testing has gone way beyond its original purview. Today it enjoys widespread use as a selection and evaluation tool for ordinary corporate employees. This use has generated a firestorm of controversy among capable job candidates, who despite their obvious qualifications, are being screened out from jobs they otherwise could handle with ease. Because this tool has been appropriated by HR fannullones with their slanted agenda, you cannot, under any circumstances, simply roll up your sleeves and unmindfully take personality tests or go unprepared into an interview with a clinical psychologist. That way disaster lies. Preparation is key.

Play along with me for a moment and indicate whether you agree, disagree, or are uncertain about the following observations:

1. I was reared by a single mother

2. I enjoy spending evenings home alone

3. I would rather grow flowers in my garden than watch the NFL Super Bowl.

If you answered "yes" to any of the statements listed above, as far as the fannullones are concerned, you're unfit for a future in Corporate America. But if you were reared in a fatherless home, as so many young men and women are today, you risk flunking the test. If you prefer gardening to watching the NFL Super Bowl you risk flunking the test. If you prefer staying home in the evenings to a rousing night of boozing with the boys, you risk flunking the test. Those examples show you just how ridiculous personality tests have become. And it doesn't speak wonders for the psychos who designed the tests or the fannulones who use them so joyfully and without restraint.

Psychological testers claim to purge "unacceptable" candidates for employment, and I imagine sometimes they do. But they also eliminate any number of highly qualified men and women who would otherwise be tremendous assets to their companies (the "throwing out the baby with the bath water" syndrome). And since very few HR fannullones are trained in psychology, they accept at face value what the psychological testers and clinical psychologists tell them.

The fact that many questions asked in psychological tests are humiliating and dehumanizing is bad enough, but what's worse is that psychological testing is accepted in thousands of businesses throughout the country. Any aspiring corporate executive who changes jobs can expect to run afoul of psychological testing sooner or later, probably sooner. Even if you're not in the job market you are not immune. Many companies use personality tests to evaluate the promotional potential of its existing employees. Yet another dangerous game that has ruined the careers of capable performers because they don't measure up to patently absurd standards.

Your only recourse is to learn to beat the testers at their own game.

It can be done if you'll follow a couple of simple rules: First, never underrate the ingenuity and deceptiveness of the shrinks and their tests. Second, learn what they consider safe and acceptable answers - and always provide them. If necessary, lie without hesitation. Otherwise you risk getting your ass booted out the corporate door. In Uncle Anastasio's vernacular: Give the wrong answer and your chances of acceptance are as good as a chipmunk fighting a Rottweiler and coming out on top.

As an aid to understanding and passing psychological tests, The Association is supplying you with two books on the subject: Martin L. Gross' The Brain Watchers (New York, Random House, 1962) and Edward Hoffman's Ace the Corporate Personality Test (New York, McGraw-Hill, 2000). Any normally intelligent recruit who studies both will greatly enhance his or her chances of passing personality tests and grueling personal interviews with psychologists. The advice the older book dispenses is just as valid today as it was fifty years ago, but the newer one is more in tune with today's trends. Study both.

Psyching Out the Psychologist

Personally, I've been through the psychological testing mills about a half-dozen times; I'm a scarred and weary veteran of personality and ink blot battles. I've learned not only how to cheat to my advantage on the tests, but also how to hold up under the intense pressure of a two-hour in-depth interview with a clinical psychologist.

Psychologists, even more than HR interviewers, are trained to detect lies during interviews. The secret to successful lying rests with your ability to believe the bullshit you spew forth while sitting face to face with the shrinks. Success comes from anticipating questions and rehearsing your answers until you've got them down cold. At that stage the expected answers become ingrained. Your confidence will soar when the shrink asks questions and you give him the answers he wants to hear. But don't get complacent. Complacency breeds sloppiness and sloppiness causes you to make mistakes.

Keep in mind that the shrink will be examining your behavior closely to spot what he thinks are tells (clues that reveal you're embellishing a fact or outright lying). Here are some of the tells that give you away:

- A change in the speed of your speech, especially going from slow to fast, in response to a question about some part of your past you don't want revealed.

- A rise in the pitch of your voice when replying to a specific question, again because the question is getting uncomfortably close to a secret part of your past.

- Twisting around in your seat or turning slightly away from the shrink when the subject of the interview shifts from mundane questions to more probing questions.

- Averting your gaze from the shrink when he asks a specific question or mentions a specific subject of something you're trying to hide.

- Nervous movements of hands or feet; excessive eye blinking.

There are other tells, and by themselves they do not necessarily indicate a pattern of lies, but why arouse the shrink's suspicions? That may cause him to delve deeper into your background. You sure as hell don't want that. Your best bet during the interview is to speak slowly and deliberately, but not so slowly as to have him think you're an idiot. Keep your eyes on his face and sit back in your chair in a relaxed position.

One of my tricks is to be long-winded and speak in a monotone. The more I talk like that the more prone the listener is to nod off. When I see the shrink's eyelids start to droop I know I've hit pay dirt. I may bore him to tears but I've also convinced him that I'm just another well-adjusted corporate drone - exactly what HR wants. I know I've stated this before, yet it bears repeating: Neither the shrinks nor the HR fannullones welcome mavericks. Conformity equates to acceptance.

It's always instructive to learn from somebody who failed the tests and why. As I described in Section One of this handbook (Shitcanned and Desperate: Anatomy of a Loser), studying failures is a good way to understand how to be successful. Here's a story told me by a guy who once worked for me, an industrial engineer:

"In my first experience with the testers I - a simple guy, straight from the hills of Tennessee, unsophisticated and trusting - was naively unaware that the best answers to questions on personality tests should always indicate a conventional, run-of-the-mill, pedestrian personality. I didn't realize that you were an "immature" manager if you:

1. Liked books and music more than sports.

2. Placed family before job.

3. Loved your mother just as much as your father. (Guaranteed if you were reared in a fatherless home, you'll never pass the personality tests, unless you lie like a son-of-a-bitch!)

4. Like to do things differently. This last one is the kiss of death to a shrink attempting to expose so-called unconventional thinkers.

To continue my story, several years ago I interviewed with a large international company located in New York. The position, in corporate industrial engineering, had a lot of top-management visibility and I was eager to get the job. I knew intuitively that the corporate industrial engineering manager liked me and respected what I accomplished for my previous employer. Only one obstacle remained: to pass the company's personality tests.

"I made an appointment with the company's clinical psychologist and subsequently endured the personality tests which, as I recall, lasted four grueling hours. They threw everything at me. Since I had found an old copy of The Brain Watchers and studied it, and because I faithfully applied what I learned on the tests - I lied through my fucking teeth - I knew I had done well.

So far, so good.

Finally, for the last two hours of the day I was scheduled for an in-depth interview with the company's resident psychologist. The interview went superbly. Applying my newly learned knowledge once more, I was able to field her questions and realized that I was on my way to becoming a new member of the company's management team. But the psychological testers never let up (a crucial point I didn't pay enough attention to), and this lady was no exception.

During the final fifteen minutes, and seemingly as an afterthought on her part, she smilingly said that there was only one other little thing she wanted me to do - write a one-paragraph story about my home life.

I don't need to tell you I was well prepared for that one. In fact, I was half expecting it. But I was cocky and off guard. Feeling that I already won the war I quickly began writing my story while the psychologist watched me.

Honest to God, her eyes bugged out and she shot a long thin finger accusingly at the paper in front of me.

"You're printing, you're not writing. I clearly told you to write a story."

I couldn't believe my ears and desperately tried to recover: "I always print. When I took mechanical drawing in college I was trained to print, and I guess it's habit now."

She picked up the paper and examined it closely. Then smiled and concluded the interview.

One week later I received a letter from the company's Human Resources Manager stating that the job was filled by another applicant. He needn't have bothered writing.

I was really disappointed. Thinking, however, that I could salvage something from the experience, I called the corporate industrial engineering manager and pressed him to find out the psychologist's findings. Because the manager was basically a decent guy - and since he didn't have to put it in writing and commit himself: always an important CYA[14] point in corporate America - he told me. The psychologist decided that printing rather than writing longhand as she instructed me to do revealed an inability to follow simple directions. That, she claimed, exposed me as a rebel likely to generate dissatisfaction among my peers and problems for my superiors. I was dropped faster than a burning charcoal at a backyard barbecue.

What absolute horseshit! I appealed the decision to the corporate industrial engineering Manager in a letter, but there was nothing he could do unless he wanted to challenge the power of his HR contemporaries. And, having little to gain he wasn't about to do that.

"Since then I've learned never to drop my guard with the God-players. Now I stay on my toes right up to the last menacing second."

Proving yet again the damaging influence of psychological testing. In hiring and promotion decisions, as my dear old Uncle Anastasio might say, it's about as useless as teats on a boar hog, but keep in mind that boar hogs are always dangerous.

Strategies from Section Four

1. Much controversy surrounds personality testing. Still, HR managers love it because it's enveloped in an atmosphere of science (pseudo-science is more like it) and provides yet another tool to screen out job candidates. For this reason alone you cannot simply take the tests without adequate preparation coupled with an understanding of what constitutes failure.

2. Personality testing, originally meant to detect sociopaths admitted to mental hospitals, is now being used to evaluate the potential of first line supervisors, middle managers and executives, as well as job candidates. Throughout your career you must stay up-to-date on what it takes to pass personality tests with flying colors. And not only for job interviews. Companies routinely spring personality tests and psychological evaluations on its supervisors, managers and executives. Consider lying de rigueur.

3. The Association has identified two books to help you prepare satisfactory responses to questions on personality tests and in-depth interviews with clinical psychologists. It's mandatory that all management recruits get copies and study them assiduously. The Association will provide you with copies of both. They are Martin L. Gross' The Brain Watchers (New York, Random House, 1962) and Edward Hoffman's Ace the Corporate Personality Test (New York, McGraw-Hill, 2000).

4. Pay special attention to face-to-face interviews with clinical psychologists. Do not underestimate how clever they can be in detecting embellishments and outright lies. Prepare not only your anticipated answers to questions, but also your behavior during the interview.

SECTION FIVE

The Association's First Management Commandment

You will have no loyalty other than to yourself, respect no counsel other than your own, and have no close friends at work.

(Note: This section and the following nine describe ten management commandments to guide your journey through Corporate America. They constitute your bible. Study them, adopt them, use them wisely, make them part of you. They specify behaviors and methodologies you must embrace to succeed in your corporate endeavors. The Association did not come across these lightly. After months of study, careful deliberation and indeed, passionate arguments, members of The Association's ruling council unanimously selected them as core values. It is essential you now make them yours.)

"Executives reward employees who are loyal to their companies, rely on bosses and peers for advice and counsel, give it freely in return and treat fellow employees as trusted associates and friends."

Every time I hear that grab bag of dubious advice I realize that bullshit is alive and flourishing in America's corporate heartland, and that many unsuspecting marks still subscribe to its Pollyannaish notions. Follow that advice and I guarantee your failure. I could cite example after example of naïve employees who talked too openly to the wrong people and found themselves in hot water, naïve employees who trusted fellow employees only to be stabbed in the back, and naïve employees who were loyal to their companies only to be discarded like garbage after years of faithful service when their jobs were shipped overseas. The simple truth is that lone wolves (people like you who must keep to themselves) fare better than corporate sheep - naïve employees who follow The Golden Rule.[15]

Employees who rely on loyalty from their companies do not truly grasp the nature of their corporate relationship. Companies pay employees for services rendered, but when those services no longer suit the needs of employers, corporations terminate those services. No ifs, no ands, no buts.

A corporation is an impersonal entity whose charter is clear: increasing sales and profits, not making nice. Nice doesn't play well on Wall Street or Main Street. Your job in Corporate America is no different than your former job back home. Mobsters and corporate managers follow the same imperative: perform or lose your valuable standing, your livelihood and possibly your lives (the latter a distinct possibility if you fuck-up grievously or, God forbid, you betray your Family. But I'm sure you already knew that).

Loyalty means getting the job done. Period. Then, and only then, does The Association reward your loyalty. I can't emphasize this enough. Failure is not an option.

Loyalty is something companies profess to honor, but in actual practice seldom do. Corporate decisions invariably come down to profit and loss, to dollars and cents, to costs vs. benefits. It's the way capitalist business operates. During your long corporate journey you must be loyal only to yourself[16] because loyalty is rarely a two-way street, and to pay homage to it is a career-busting mistake. A mistake you cannot afford to make.

This is a radical departure from the way you conducted business at home with your respective families. There, loyalty to your Family extended to fellow "soldiers" since you were all together in crime. If one fell, others were likely to follow. So you had to close ranks. In times of great stress (pursuit by the law, for example) everybody pulled together. In Corporate America you will be a lone sentinel; on your own.

The same maxim that says play your cards close to your chest when dealing with bosses, holds true for your relationships with peers and subordinates. Your trusted associate at work could morph into your worst enemy tomorrow if it becomes a matter of who leaves and who remains in a layoff, or who gets promoted and who gets left behind. The Golden Rule falls by the wayside when shit hits the fan.

Smart corporate players know they have little choice but to respect their own counsel above all. To share one's innermost feelings and desires and plans with others in an environment where fierce competition dominates is to invite envy and retaliation. Smart corporate players do not reveal their playing cards to anybody at work; they shun close associations that could backfire and harm their careers. An old boss of our Family once advised me many years ago, "In a business like ours, only those who know how to keep their mouths shut and eyes and ears open make it to old age. The rest get early funerals, fancy caskets and lots of flowers."

Examples

The following story illustrates the weak bond between company and employee, even when the employee has worked his heart and soul out for his company. I heard this story at a bar one evening after Matt, the civilian[17] who told me his sad tale, had downed one too many martinis.

From what I could piece together, Matt worked thirty-five years for his company as a pharmaceutical scientist. He topped out as a low-level manager because his talents and desires ran more toward technology than management. Executives recognized Matt's strengths, and more important, his failings, so they reassigned him to a lab position where his main job involved developing new chemical compounds. Matt picks up the story:

> "It took me a long time to discover that my skills and the kind of work I felt comfortable with were technical. I'm happiest around beakers and test tubes and Bunsen burners. There are too many headaches supervising people, so I stepped down from a management position and went back to the lab working as a senior scientist.
>
> I joined the company right out of college and, unlike many of my classmates, I stayed with the same company my entire career. I was very loyal and over the years developed several new chemical compounds that translated into increased sales and profits for the company.
>
> When my boss called me into his office one Friday afternoon and told me I had to take a thirty percent pay cut and be reassigned as a menial lab assistant or take early retirement, I darn near fell off my chair. I was counting on working another four years at my current compensation level to increase my pension.

Since the most important years for building pension money are your last five or so, the effect of the pay cut or early retirement would be to wipe away thirty percent of the money I was counting on. Without that extra monthly income, my wife, Jane, and I would be forced to skimp during our golden years.

"To make a long story short, the company didn't return the loyalty I showed it. I felt betrayed. I left that same Friday without saying goodbye to all those people I worked with over the years. I never went back. Now my only contact with them is through my lawyer. I'm suing the bastards."

Poor naïve Matt found out too late that the concept of loyalty, beguiling as it appears to be, no longer exists, if it ever did to begin with. He believed the company screwed him over as a reward for his thirty-five years of loyal service but he had it all wrong. Matt failed to recognize that the implicit contract between company and employee is dictated by necessity as the company sees it, not as the employee desires it. When the company no longer needs an employee it cuts the bond. Had Matt's perspective been more grounded, he would have taken the precaution over the years to build his nest egg accordingly, knowing that the axe might fall at any moment. Surely he noticed other employees bitterly complaining about losing their jobs or getting demoted unfairly. That should have alerted him to the realities.

Matt was lucky to even receive a pension. Pensions are going the way of the dinosaur; they're rapidly becoming extinct. Any younger manager working in Corporate America today foolish enough to count on money coming from corporate coffers after he retires has his head up that orifice where the sun doesn't shine. It's just not going to happen for those not counted among the company's top executives.

I advise you to learn this from Matt's experience: Don't for a moment believe that your company will nourish and cherish you as The Association does, your true family; there is no large, comforting, corporate tit. Like it or not, you're on your own in Corporate America. You're in a combat zone from which few survive unscathed.

In another example that demonstrates The Association's first management commandment, Bob discovered how untrustworthy Rudy, his subordinate and confidant, was (demonstrating that business and personal friendships do not mix outside of The Association). The pair, who often socialized together, worked for a giant technology company with a multitude of divisions. The top brass ordered Bob to cut his costs and Bob decided to curtail one of his major projects, the one Rudy headed. It was an honest decision and while Bob felt bad about downsizing Rudy's responsibilities, he decided he had no other choice but to go ahead. He advised Rudy to start looking around the company for another position (a standard practice for executives in this mammoth company that plays musical chairs more often than the original TV game show). He admonished Rudy not to discuss the subject with Bob's boss, Pete. In fact he gave him a direct order to bypass Pete in his quest for a new position.

Rudy called several of his former bosses. Despite instructions, one of the executives he contacted was Pete. Rudy then did the unforgivable: Despite Bob's admonition he told Pete that his project was being mothballed. Pete flew into a rage. The project was one that Pete started years ago and wanted to expand, not contract, and didn't sly Rudy know it. He counted on Pete running interference for him and of course it worked. Pete instructed Bob to keep the project running and he wasn't too nice about how he told him. The upshot was that Rudy remained on the job but lost Bob's confidence. Rudy's diarrhea of the mouth was stupid, the kind of mistake smart corporate players never make. Rudy made an enemy of an influential executive; that's the first big no no in the smart player's career management handbook.

Needless to say, Rudy's betrayal stung Bob and it taught him the hard way to keep work associates and personal friends separate, and to always maintain an arm's distance from fellow employees. Bob eventually squeezed Rudy out of his division, but the damage was already done. Pete never forgave Bob, proving that once you get on somebody's shit list it's next to impossible to get off. The bottom line of this charade was two careers ruined and one top executive highly pissed-off.

Strategies from Section Five

1. Your only loyalty is to The Association. Period. Regardless of which branch you came from (Italian, Jewish, Russian, Irish), you took an oath that binds you to us forever. You owe no loyalty to the corporation we have assigned you to, other than to flourish and succeed. But even ordinary citizens who work for corporations should realize that the concept of loyalty is tenuous at best. Companies seldom feel they have any loyalty to their employees other than to reward them with a paycheck once every two weeks or once every month. It's strictly a business transaction devoid of human warmth. Only the hopelessly naive believe differently.

2. Competition for jobs and promotions in today's corporation borders on the insane, especially since the market crash of 2008. It's every man for himself. In such an environment only a fool looks for friends. Allies with common interests, yes; personal friends no. You never know when somebody might use something you said or did against you. Meaning keep your guard up. Treat everybody you work with as a potential adversary or spy. That attitude will shield you from doing or saying something stupid. The Association does not reward stupidity.

3. Watch your back; it's perpetually in danger of being stabbed. Trust nobody. In the example shown immediately above, Bob trusted Rudy and was rewarded with a stiletto between the shoulder blades. He treated him as a confidante, not thinking

that Rudy would go running to Bob's boss and object to shutting down the project he was working on. A better alternative would have been for Bob to let his boss know before Rudy got to him, thereby allowing him the opportunity to slant the decision in his favor.

4. If you feel the need to confide in anybody or get advice, the door to The Association is open twenty-four/seven. You each have an Association contact, a mentor who has pledged to aid you, whenever you need him and for whatever reason. Take advantage of this close relationship. As the old saying goes, No man (or woman)is an island.

SECTION SIX

The Association's Second
Management Commandment

You Will Be as Ruthless as Attila the Hun

Attitude, as they say is everything. If your attitude reflects the willingness to accept sub-par performance from yourself as well as from subordinates, your job performance will suffer and opportunities for advancement will evaporate faster than smoke in a hurricane.

Employees are quick to spot this weakness - for that's what it is - and exploit it. Subordinates slack off, jealous peers mount vicious attacks against you and the executives in your company consider you unfit for command. You'll embarrass your sponsor, The Association. The bosses back home keep tabs of your progress or lack of it (they have operatives everywhere monitoring your performance), and if they suspect you're not tough enough to endure the corporate struggle, your career is in jeopardy. Once they believe you don't have what it takes to make it to the top of your company, they'll pluck you off the job faster than a baseball manager yanks a weak pitcher in the ninth inning of a tie ballgame. You're then deader than roadkill.

The fact is that nobody really likes or respects weakness, even when that weakness is based on acts of kindness. Kindness is for kiddies, not striving employees, hungry to reach the top. And it's definitely not for Association management recruits, not after all the time and money invested in you.

When it comes to getting the job done you must be as ruthless as Attila the Hun. For those of you who are history-deprived, Attila was the victorious fifth-century leader of an empire stretching from Germany and

Eastern Europe well into Russia. He led an army considered to be one of the most bloodthirsty and rapacious in history. Attila spared nobody when it came to achieving his military and political objectives, no matter how many bodies he left littered on the battlefield. And he left them by the thousands.

Transferring this no-nonsense attitude to your job means not accepting any excuse for sub-standard performance. It doesn't help if Danny, a subordinate who is disabled and a hell of a nice guy, gets his work out ninety percent of the time and you forgive the ten percent lapse due to his disability, perhaps even praise his overall effort, in a misguided attempt at commiseration. If you're to succeed, it's the ten percent you'll be concerned about because it's causing you to miss goals. The milk of human kindness curdles in a cutthroat business environment where bosses respond to your lax performance with frowns and scowls . . . and pink slips.

Find some foolishly sympathetic manager who will take Danny off your hands, somebody compassionate and understanding. Better his performance suffer than yours. Sure, top management will publicly applaud Danny's new manager for his "humanity" - it's the politically correct thing to do - but come promotion time, that manager will eat your dust. Better believe it. Top management doesn't tolerate excuses; it loves nothing better than ruthless strivers willing to do whatever it takes to get the job done, regardless of what that entails. Not much different than The Association's business, is it? We're more physical, corporation executives more subtle (every demotion and firing covered by a smile), but the end result is the same.

If you can't find a sympathetic manager in your company (a distinct possibility. Smart managers hate to get saddled with inefficient employees, no matter how tragic their circumstances), your remaining alternative is to fire Danny. Using Attila the Hun as your guide, ask yourself, if he were in your place, would he allow Danny to interfere with his performance? Bet your ass he wouldn't. It's off with Danny's head. If that shocks or offends you, close this book right now and pick up Winnie the Pooh. You are not Association - or corporate executive - material.

Examples

Over drinks at a business conference, a manager of industrial engineering for a Southern textile mill confided in me about an important project that upper management assigned him. A make or break project for his career, and he was well aware of the consequences of failing. His future with the company hung in the balance.

The guy was drunk and blabbing his mouth off. Since I'm a sympathetic listener, I get to hear all manner of corporate horror stories, especially in airport bars where businessmen, no last names exchanged, swap confidences and unload their venom. Anyway, here's what he told me:

> "The project involved installing a new statistical control software system on knitting machines to improve quality output. My group was directly

responsible for installing the statistical charts and control reports, while Information Systems (IS), another department under the supervision of a peer, was responsible for developing the statistical control software for us to install. The plant manager handed me overall responsibility for bringing the project in on schedule and at budgeted costs.

Ray, the manager of the IS department, and I were competitors for promotion. This new project would give me a leg up and Ray sure as hell wasn't going to allow it. He did everything possible to stonewall so the project lagged. No matter how I tried to persuade him that successful completion of the project was in his benefit as well as mine, he refused to cooperate.

I was running out of time to meet the schedule, so I was forced to take drastic measures. The rumor mill had it that Ray was screwing one of the clerks in his department during the lunch hour break. I stayed tuned in to grapevine rumors, because you never know when you're going to pick up a nugget of useful information. This was one of those times.

I followed Ray when he went out for lunch three successive days and observed nothing more unappetizing than Ray devouring a corned beef sandwich on rye and washing it down with a Dr. Pepper. On the fourth day I struck gold. Ray and his willing señorita headed for a cheesy motel on the seedy side of town. I followed the eager pair, took pictures of them entering and leaving the motel with my digital camera, and paid the motel clerk ten bucks to let me photograph the registration in Ray's handwriting. Ray used a fictitious name, of course, but his handwriting was unmistakable.

The next day I confronted Ray and 'persuaded' him to cooperate with me. His eyes spit bullets, but he had little choice, fearing that copies of him and his blushing señorita entering the motel and the pics showing his registration signature might find their way to our boss and to Ray's wife. I never once claimed I'd disclose them, never once threatened him in any manner, and I never would have, not in a million years. It was a bluff, because such revelations coming from me would have damaged my reputation more than Ray's, but he was too stirred up to figure that out - and too scared of me because of the lengths I went to nail his ass. So he offered no further resistance.

The project was completed on time, and from that day forward Ray never gave me any trouble. Six months later, he left for a job in another company.

In the end I rescued the project and my reputation. Ray, the uncooperative shit, didn't know what hit him."

Mary, one of my former girlfriends and manager of a one-hundred employee administrative support function in a major telecommunications company told me about the time she was forced to cut her staff by twenty percent - a hefty reduction under any circumstance.

"Arbitrary staff reductions are the hardest of all since they cut across the board. But the order came down from upstairs leaving no room for argument. My job was to make the cut and carry the existing load with twenty percent fewer clerks. No arguments and no stalling.

My three unit managers and I worked well into the night deciding who should go and who should stay. Since our administrative support function is a large one, and one of the few remaining in the States that hadn't already been transferred to India, the handwriting was on the wall. Either reduce costs or risk losing the function to some back office in Bombay.

Two of my managers argued for laying off the least senior employees, while the other argued for laying off the least productive. The seniority argument is a strong one since in times of layoffs it lessens the blow to morale and appears less capricious. It also keeps the union off our doorstep, a compelling argument we had to seriously consider since we were a non-union shop.

But laying off by seniority meant that my department would be less flexible since those employees remaining would not have the same skill sets we needed to function well. Besides, our performance level would almost certainly drop because the least senior members were our most productive. Not an attractive prospect, especially with the threat of an Indian operation looming over us. As Murphy's Law would have it, four of the twenty highest seniority employees were teetering on the edge of bankruptcy, and laying-them off meant the banks would foreclose their homes their homes if they couldn't find other work quickly.

While I wanted to be fair and impartial, I also realized that my department's job performance was riding on the outcome. As an added factor, I guessed that my boss and his boss wondered if I was strong enough to make the tough decisions. Believe me, I sure wasn't about to look bad in their eyes. I finally ruled in favor of laying-off the high seniority, least productive employees. Frankly, the other way would have devastated my career and I couldn't have that."

Attila the Hun characteristics can sometimes be carried to barbaric extremes that would do justice to more primitive Association methods. Listen to this story an associate told me:

"Years ago, I worked in an automotive company's Midwest assembly plant. One afternoon a production worker, transferring car body shells[18] with an overhead monorail hoist, was knocked-out cold when one of those body shells unexpectedly pivoted on the hoist and slapped him flush across the back of his head.

The lack of a body shell shut down the entire plant's assembly line immediately, as it was designed to do upon an unscheduled interruption.

Sirens blasted throughout every corner of the plant and offices. Nearby managers and supervisors dropped what they were doing and rushed to the location of the shutdown, as did emergency maintenance workers.

The plant production manager happened to be fairly close to the shutdown when the sirens began blaring. He hopped onto his electric cart and raced down the plant's aisles, screaming at everybody to get out of his way. He arrived at the transfer point where the production worker was lying unconscious on the floor, blood oozing from the back of his head, the monorail hoist swinging idly above his prone body.

The manager jumped off his electric cart, grabbed the arms of the unconscious worker and dragged him away from the transfer point, then raced back to and grabbed the hoist's controls. Within seconds he was feeding body shells to the line. The sirens stopped their ear-shattering blare and the assembly line lurched ahead.

Nobody paid any attention to the unconscious worker. Managers and workers, engrossed in the immediate task of restoring order to the assembly line, stepped around him as if they were avoiding an oil slick on the floor. The worker lay there for another three or four minutes until a motorized stretcher finally arrived to take him to the first aid station, where an ambulance carted him off to a local hospital. The plant production manager instructed a line helper to wipe the injured worker's blood off the floor. Other than that tiny concession to propriety, it was as if nothing had happened. Such is the environment of the assembly line, where life and limb take a back seat to production."

I would add that the devotion the production manager showed to his job - achieving his goal of planned production - is exactly the type of devotion you must apply to your job in Corporate America to succeed. You can always wipe up the blood afterward.

Strategies from Section Six

1. You must be tough-minded but soften the face you show in public. Employees in Corporate America respond to a friendly appearance and tend to accept even the harshest treatment if it comes accompanied by a smile.

2. Filter every decision you make by asking this question: How will the decision I make affect my career? Forget the number of bodies that pile up, as long as your career moves forward and upward. Many call this kind of thinking callous; The Association calls it essential, and so must you.

3. Sooner or later, somebody's going to raise the issue of how much help a management recruit can get directly from The Association. The answer: very little. You must learn to stand on your own two feet and conquer career crises. That's what makes you strong. However, in rare cases, when you're near the pinnacle of your corporation and an adversary is blocking your path to the top corporate job, The Association may lend a hand and "remove" the obstacle. But only as a matter of last resort.

4. Top executives reward tough-minded employees who focus on results; they tend to discard those who are more concerned about striking a proper balance between profits and employee welfare. The smarter players understand this intuitively. Profits always take precedence over the care and feeding of employees, but never admitted publicly.

SECTION SEVEN

The Association's Third
Management Commandment

You Will Marry a Mate Who is Clever, Ruthless and
Willing to Play Dirty to Support Your Career

When most men and women in the Western world marry, they do so for love. True, there are exceptions: to escape loneliness, to raise a family, to have regular sex (seldom a problem nowadays in an environment where sex is as common as shaking hands). People marry for love because they have bought into the notion that love conquers all. Most aspiring corporate employees do not select husbands and wives based on their ability as career helpmates. As our English brethren would say "Pity," because a tuned-in mate with an avaricious disposition can be an enormous asset for a corporate climber. As can a wealthy one, because with wealth comes connections, and connections are frequently the key to career success.

I don't have statistics to prove my point - I don't think any such statistics exist - but anecdotal evidence would suggest that employees who ignore this crucial aspect of their careers do not advance as fast or as far as those who marry ambitious and cunning mates or mates who are rich.

Helpmates offer several advantages. They:

- Gather juicy bits of information from other company wives that their husbands can use at work. (Note: this example assumes husbands are the primary breadwinners, yet it can be the other way around. For purposes of simplicity, I am using the example of a male breadwinner.)

- Plant misinformation among those same wives that is helpful to their husbands' careers and damaging to their adversaries.

- Play up their husbands' bosses to curry favor for their husbands.

- Help their husbands strategize their careers and plan on-the-job tactics to outmaneuver job opponents. A helpmate removed from the immediate combat offers an objective and valuable perspective, and often a career-saving one.

- Make connections for their husbands on their own if they hold influential jobs themselves or have influential contacts elsewhere.

The Association encourages you to marry a mate who will be helpful to your career. Management recruits with mates climb the corporate ladder faster than management recruits who undertake their corporate odysseys alone. We encourage you to select a mate from within your respective Family, but if such a mate is not available, The Association will help you locate and select the "perfect" mate for you. Prefect defined as somebody who will do anything to anybody at anytime to advance your career, but do it with nuance and refinement. Again, meat cleavers are out, machination and guile in.

Examples

Steve, ambitious manager for a large health insurance company, married well. His wife, Gwen, reared by a struggling lower middle class family in Boston, had worked her way through college to earn a bachelor's degree in business, followed by a prestigious Harvard MBA. A top level national consulting hired her and she worked for it until turning twenty-eight and marrying Steve. From then on she devoted herself to helping him move ahead.

Gwen had the polish and sophistication required to walk among the elite. Yet underneath that cultured veneer she was a gutter fighter who offered no quarter.

In many respects Steve was her twin. Raised in a fatherless Midwest home, he worked his way through college and quickly rose through the ranks to an upper middle management position by the time he reached thirty. So the marriage between Steve and Gwen was a natural.

Steve was on the brink of becoming a vice president, the youngest in the health insurance company's history. His only job competition came from George, another young comer in the organization. Their abilities and accomplishments were so close that Steve worried he might lose out to George if he didn't take some action to upstage his capable rival. He and his wife, Gwen, put their heads together.

Gwen did the research. She studied George's background and made a dossier that focused on his weaknesses, which she and Steve had to admit, weren't many. Undeterred, she dug up information that George had bought a second home at a lakeside community seventy-five miles from work, a home that he and his family planned to live in on weekends. Steve and Gwen knew that one of the company's chief competitors was headquartered near that same community.

In the short time Gwen and Steve had been married, Gwen had nurtured her relationship with Janet, the wife of Steve's boss. The ladies hit it off (Gwen made sure of that) and felt comfortable exchanging tidbits of gossip with each other. At a country club dinner party a week or so after Gwen had uncovered the information about George's lakeside home, she and Janet strolled into the garden after dinner. The ensuing conversation went something like this:

"I hear you've bought a lakeside home," Gwen said, and sipped her cocktail.

Janet's brow furrowed. "Not Pete and me. Where'd you hear that?"

Gwen pursed her lips for a moment; then her face brightened. "You're right, it wasn't you. It was George and Stella." (George's wife)

"Oh, I wasn't aware of that," Janet said. "What are they doing living there? That's quite a distance from work."

"Seventy-five miles."

Janet arched an eyebrow. "He isn't planning to commute that distance every day, is he?"

"It is an awfully long commute. One-hundred-fifty miles a day."

Janet clicked her tongue. "Doesn't make any sense, does it?"

"Janet, I honestly don't know what to say. All I know about the lakeside community where George and Stella live: it's home to another big insurance company."

Janet frowned. "Yes, I know. Our largest rival."

"Oh, goodness," Gwen said, "I hope I haven't let the cat out of the bag."

Ah, Gwen, all innocence. In one brilliantly executed thrust she created doubts about George's intentions to remain with the company. Janet, a skilled corporate wife anxious to protect her husband, wasn't about to allow that juicy piece of information to go unattended. She passed the information on to her husband. Although Pete - no stranger himself to corporate scheming - understood Gwen's motive, he nevertheless was concerned. Even after he discovered that the lakeside home would not be George's primary residence, Pete was unsure about George's intentions. That was compounded by his fear that George might someday bolt to his company's main competitor and reveal confidential product and market information. If Pete promoted George and if George later took a powder, Pete would have looked foolish in the eyes of the company's CEO. He couldn't afford that. Steve got the promotion.

In another example Mark, senior vice president of sales and marketing for a graphics company, married Laura, a marketing manager with his company who worked in another division. Laura was up for promotion but it looked as if John, an advertising manager in Laura's division, and her main adversary, would get the job. John was a rising star in the company and much admired by the company's top executives.

Mark realized that Laura didn't have much of a chance competing against John, so what he did was lure John into his division as a vice president, which left his wife Laura without any real opposition. She was shortly afterward promoted to marketing vice president.

Everybody was happy except Mark who knew that eventually John would constitute a threat to his position. Of course, Mark and Laura had planned carefully for this. They dug deep into John's background, attempting to uncover some damaging information that could sideline him. And discovered that John once had a tawdry affair with a man, a real career buster in Corporate America where the faintest taint of a gay sex scandal sends everybody ducking for cover. Do I have to mention that Mark and Laura made sure that information surfaced. Without their name attached to it, of course. Needless to say, that exposure tarnished John's otherwise sterling reputation, thereby ending the threat. Poor John, he never knew what hit him.

Strategies from Section Seven

1. A clever wife who will stop at nothing to help you succeed can advance your career by leaps and bounds. She has endless opportunities from planting misinformation about your job adversary with the boss's wife to sidling up to the big boss himself and working her charms. Some wives start affairs with influential executives to promote their husbands' careers. If your wife can handle that scene, guess who's going to win the next promotion? I can assure you it won't be your job adversary.

2. It's not up to The Association to determine if your wife should step over the line to help her husband, but in matters of career advancement, who determines where that line is? The Association certainly will not be disappointed if her seduction results in your ascension up the corporate ladder at warp speed. After all, infidelity is a relative matter. It bothers some; others take it in stride. The decision rests with you and your wife, but I would advise you to use whatever weapons you have available in your pursuit of the ultimate prize. The Association will applaud you for it.

3. As you can tell from the previous point, in the race to the top of the corporate pyramid anything goes, provided you don't get caught.

4. You cannot view your wife's efforts to help you through the prism of what's considered acceptable behavior in current society. After all, if you can slip the knife to your adversaries you'll do it without hesitation. Why should you want your wife to be any different? If your delicate sensibilities urge you to say 'not for me', perhaps that's a sign you may find the brutal adversarial reality of corporate life too stressful to handle.

5. It helps if you marry for money. A wife with contacts, especially money contacts, can do you a world of good. Money men and women control the purse strings of Corporate America and as such call the shots. Getting the money people on your side is a fast ticket to the executive suite.

SECTION EIGHT

The Association's Fourth
Management Commandment

You Will Use Whatever Deception Necessary
to Avoid Job Assignments Where the
Probability of Success is Low

Since I joined the business world I have watched one hard-charging executive after another take any random job assignment that comes along without adequately thinking it through, thereby tossing his or her fate to the wind. Most who do are younger, inexperienced and unaware of the career dangers some assignments pose. Others subscribe to the belief that any assignment can succeed if only one works hard enough. This misconception is a hidden trap that sidelines careers, one you must take every caution to avoid.

Sure, it's easy to say risk taking is part and parcel of corporate life. That's true, but there are two categories of risk taking: one where the risks are known and one where the risks are unknown. It's the latter category that destroys promising careers.

Think back to your days in organized crime. You didn't leave the outcome of your work to fate, did you? You took every means to assure that you completed your assignments fully and on time. If you ran a protection business and one of your "customers" balked at paying his dues, you cracked heads, thereby minimizing the risk you would suffer a cash shortfall on his account. It's the same principle in business but one without the application of physical force. Brutality remains an option, of course, but only in extreme circumstances and only with prior Association approval. The point is if you must rely on physical force to resolve an issue, somehow you missed the boat at an earlier stage when you incorrectly assessed the risks. Smart corporate players do not operate blind. They take risks when they have to and avoid those where the probability of success is unknown.

Let's digress for a moment to talk about threats and force in relation to corporate adversaries. Usually you will be well-positioned to move ahead of any adversary from instructions you find in this manual. But when an exceptional adversary poses substantive risks to your career, veiled threats may carry the day, especially if your opponent, man or woman, displays signs of weakness. A little fear goes a long way to neutralizing a corporate opponent who is unaccustomed to anything more violent than an approaching thunderstorm.

But take care. It's not acceptable corporate behavior to threaten anybody (although top-floor executives love nothing better than aggressive managers who will stop at virtually nothing to get the job done. It's just not politically correct to express that preference). Cunning and deceit constitutes the preferred behavior in Corporate America. They will protect you from accusations of overly aggressive behavior. But when you need to use threats, make your adversary understand the perils of challenging your ascendency and the folly of reporting you for threatening him. I'm sure you learned how in your former position with the mob.

Getting back to our discussion of risks, understand that anything new carries risks. Many new assignments have hidden traps. Those risks and traps may not be immediately apparent. If they were, aspiring executives would not be so eager to pounce. Here is a sample list of potentially unknown problems you might face when tackling new assignments:

- The new assignment may be the wet dream of some idiot executive, but if the venture fails, he won't lose his job, you will.

- Resources available for the new assignment may be inadequate. You can't build a house without bricks and mortar, or a new product or division without an adequate budget. Foolish "heroes" may attempt to, but they'll inevitably burn out and crash.

- Employees with the technical background needed for new assignments may be scarce and overpriced.

- As described in a previous chapter, a new company function may be considerably less costly when operated in a third world country, but top executives will often start it at home first to iron out bugs and establish standard procedures. They may hide their true intentions from you, leaving you without a job when the company transfers the operation overseas.

Well, you get the idea. There are all manner of potential traps awaiting you on a new job assignment. You're going to be dazzled by the promotion, the extra money, the attention you're receiving from the brass and accolades from The Association. All of these inducements are heady distractions that could spell trouble if you don't take the needed time and thought to determine the risks and hidden traps beforehand.

Yet it's not always easy ferreting out potential pitfalls and assessing their severity. There are two components to this dilemma:

1. Determining the risks themselves.

2. Deciding on your response; learning how to turn down assignments without damaging your career if you regard them as too uncertain and fraught with risk.

Both steps require forethought and stealth. The first, determining the risks, is relatively straightforward. You need an ally in the know. If you already have a corporate sponsor high up in the company, she may be able to tip you off to any shortcomings of the assignment. If you don't have your rabbi in place, shame on you. You didn't absorb the basic lesson from Section Two of this handbook. By now it may be too late.

You may need somebody, other than a rabbi, who has insights into the project, possibly a technical guru who has the ability to evaluate the technological risks. Or a marketing expert who understands what customers are looking for if the assignment involves developing new markets. Or a financial whiz who can spot cost hazards if the margins are low. And so on. The basic requirement is that the person or persons you enlist in your cause must be germane to the assignment and willing and able to provide insights.

Once you've located the absolutely best person in the know, you'll need to "persuade" him that it's to his advantage to help you. If you have a reputation as a comer in the company, somebody with power, your target may readily cooperate. If you don't yet have that power, you may need to take steps similar to those I described in Section Two - locating an appropriate sponsor and finding common ground with your target, then exploiting the relationship (with any luck it may not be too late in the day). Or it may take the form of paying off the helper with a favor of your own. Lasting relationships are often forged through quid pro quo arrangements. In a few instances, an outright offer of cash may buy you an ally, but handle this carefully less you are accused of bribing a fellow employee. If you get impatient you may be tempted to resort to strong-arm tactics, but as I mentioned before, that's a perilous gambit. If any of your corporate bosses discover your predilection to violence your career is effectively over. Consider strong-arm tactics as a last gasp desperate attempt. And then take steps to assure that your target doesn't spill his guts to the wrong people.

Regardless of the approach chosen, it's up to you to decide what works best. That takes homework, and often a lot of it. But since your career is on the line, the hard work is justified. After all, who is the most important person of all? It's you, baby. So go for it.

Assuming the new assignment is a dog, a project with a dim future, your next move is to turn it down without damaging your reputation with the brass. The following example describes one approach that works. It may suggest other possibilities.

Example

Gordon, the cost accounting manager for a machinery manufacturer, was in a spot.

"Just like anybody else, I was ambitious, and probably a touch over-eager, because I think my boss felt threatened by me. At the time, I was a twenty-six-year-old go-getter, and Toby my boss, a fifty-five-year-old financial manager who had topped out. He wasn't going anywhere. I knew it, he knew it. Everybody in Accounting and Finance knew it.

In sneaky, underhanded ways he tried to make me look bad. For example, come annual inventory time, he'd assign me and my crew the dirtiest jobs in the inventory, counting thousands of machined parts scattered across the production floor. It was hard getting an accurate count and he'd blame me when the count didn't match inventory records.

In other ways, Toby found how to make my life miserable. Nothing I could ever bitch about. He was too clever for that. But he was forever pecking away at me, hoping I'm sure, that I would either ask for reassignment to another department or resign from the company. Nothing worked. I clung on tenaciously and managed somehow to counter Toby's moves such that my reputation with the brass wasn't damaged.

"Finally, Toby came up with what I imagine he thought was a perfect solution. He created a new position in his department, one dedicated to identifying and reducing overhead costs, and he wanted me to fill it. Identifying high costs is something cost accounting people do well. That's our job. But not reducing them, because overhead costs are principally controlled by the manufacturing and engineering departments. In essence, Toby was positioning me to fail.

I had to think fast. What I did was propose that the job be given to Geneva, a young, bright and ambitious industrial engineer, a black woman. She worked in the manufacturing area and not only was she an expert in cost reduction, she also had an encyclopedic knowledge of manufacturing costs. The job would be a promotion and an opportunity to make a name for herself.

Needless to say Toby shit a brick when I proposed Geneva's name. I told him she could do the job better than anyone else he could think of, including me. He turned down my recommendation, as I knew he would.

Fortunately, I had cultivated a relationship with the vice president of manufacturing by going out of my way to supply him with information to help him run his departments. Back door, of course, and without Toby's knowledge. When I told him about the new job Toby proposed, he enthusiastically supported my recommendation of Geneva. Since the VP was one of the company big wheels he prevailed over Toby, whom top management considered an old fuddy duddy, anyway. Of course, it didn't hurt to sort of whisper in the VP's ear that perhaps Toby wasn't high on black people. I'm sure that helped seal the deal. Dirty? Yeah, but Toby never should have fucked me over. After that, I owed him nothing.

I don't have to tell you, and I'm sure you can see what's coming - six months later Toby 'retired' and I got his job."

Sort of leaves you with the impression that Gordon's going right to the top, and pity the poor bastard who stands in his way, doesn't it? No crappy job assignments for that boy. Gordon possesses the mindset you must have to survive and flourish in Corporate America.

Strategies from Section Eight

1. It's your responsibility to assess the chances of success or failure of all job assignments before accepting them. That means anticipating the risks before your boss assigns you. After that, it's too late.

2. This is probably one of the more difficult tasks facing you because it's not always easy to see what's around the next corner. You can prepare by learning to play chess. The game helps you predict your opponent's move and plan a couple of steps ahead. It will expand your ability to assess job assignments. And it carries the added benefit of teaching you how to outthink your job rival. Do not underestimate the difficulty of assessing risk. It's not always easy to forecast potential assignment pitfalls, because some of them come from left field, but it's important that you sharpen your insights. Intimate familiarity with your area of expertise is essential.

3. Stay in close touch with the people in your company who evaluate the potential of new products, services and markets. And I'm not talking about the top echelon of those departments. I mean the grunts: the guys and gals on the firing line who are intimately familiar with the difficulties of launching new product lines or opening new markets. More often than not, they'll be intimately familiar with the pitfalls and shortcomings of the company's latest project

the top bosses may be unaware of. Don't forget the human factor: Top executives sponsoring the project will not want to hear bad news about their pet project and they'll cut off any debate about its shortcomings. So asking them for their opinion may be counterproductive. The people on the firing line have no such axe to grind.

4. Once you've identified possible assignments, study every possible aspect to determine if they're feasible. If not, prepare your excuses well ahead of time so they don't look like excuses.

SECTION NINE

The Association's Fifth
Management Commandment

You will spy on bosses, peers and
subordinates, because information is king,
inside information a kingdom

To naïve employees who adhere to The Golden Rule, nothing is quite as offensive as spying, whether it's on subordinates, peers or bosses. Those same purists condemn the CIA for spying on America's enemies under the naive assumption that Marquis of Queensberry rules govern fair play among nations. Regrettably, The Golden Rule is not practiced by nations nor by corporations (although both will claim otherwise). That doesn't deter The Golden Rule mindset, which refuses to accept scripture not matching its own impossibly lofty standards of ethical behavior.

Failure to uncover dirt on people they work with deprives purists of valuable insights needed to control subordinates, upstage adversaries and manage bosses. As the smart corporate player knows intuitively, control is everything; without it ambitious employees cast their fate to the winds. Like it or not, spying is a necessary means to that end.

Spying is by no means confined to the corporate world. It's alive and flourishing in other organizations such as churches, academia, non-profit organizations, unions and governmental bodies where its practice has been honed razor sharp over the years. Ascending any hierarchy, wherever it is, takes a certain degree of gamesmanship and cunning. Not to play the game is to give your adversaries, who do play the game, a leg up in the race to succeed.

Getting the dirt on anybody today is a snap. Here are a few ideas or sources that might suggest others:

Search public documents such as birth and marriage records, credit reports, property records and criminal histories. This information is readily available from a variety of online sources, and gathering it is legal. You can either pay somebody to do it for you (for example, Complete Criminal Records $19 as advertised online) or dig it out yourself. You might, alternatively, contact The Association and let them work their sources to obtain the information you need. Hey, maybe you'll find that your main adversary at work was a convicted cat burglar. Think he put that on his job application? If he didn't, wouldn't his boss like to have that juicy tidbit of information (without knowing it came from you, of course)?

Type in a target's name on Google or any other search engine and you may be surprised at what you find. Anybody who has a complaint against anybody or anything (and everybody does) voices his or her grievances online. This is a great source for personal dirt, the kind that ruins reputations. Perhaps your work adversary was once accused of shoplifting. Think you can use that against him?

Open Google Search and type in the target's e-mail address. You may be the fortunate recipient of some salacious or otherwise incriminating messages. Also, visit NetTrace (www.nettrace.com.au).

Here you'll find dozens of avenues to pursue to locate hidden information about your quarry. A test of your resourcefulness will be to use databases such as displayed here to dig up the dirt.

Could be your target is advertising for partners on a porn Website. Don't forget to try the main social networking Websites such as Facebook, Twitter and LinkedIn. You never know what you'll find.

Pay attention to the grapevine. You can often hear the most delicious gossip about your target.

Even when you're unsure about the validity of gossip, it may still be possible to use it against your adversary. Assuming the rumor is floating around out there on the grapevine, there are reasons for it. It may not be exactly true but what do you care? Start your own malicious rumor, close to the one circulating on the grapevine, but take steps to assure it can't be traced to you. After all, two rumors are better than one. Yours will substantiate the original rumor and make it even more believable.

Develop a network of informants who will feed you information useful to your career. When I was vice president of sales and marketing I chatted daily with sales clerks and customer service representatives. For my reward I received lots and lots of information (much of it titillating, some of it useful) about subordinates, peers and bosses I never would have heard elsewhere. Information that on one occasion prevented a walkout - a peer was fomenting trouble for me. I nipped the revolt in the bud. I also encouraged clerks to gripe, which helped me correct weak spots in their supervisors' performance. The supervisors hated it. But so what. It kept them on their toes and kept me abreast of developing problems. It pays to be close to the people at the bottom; they know more about what's going on than most managers and they're willing to talk freely.

Follow your target if you suspect he or she is up to no good. Amazon.com lists several books that describe how to tail people without being observed. (The good ol' Internet to the rescue, once again).

Whatever approaches you choose, be careful not to cross the line into illegality. Remember, you are not back home where criminal activities are de rigueur. When Hewlett-Packard executives discovered somebody was leaking confidential information from the boardroom, they hired private investigators who used illegal pretexting - gaining access to other people's personal records under false pretenses - to discover the culprit. That act brought down the company's top executive officer.

Example

Miranda, the woman telling the following story is now one of our management recruits, one of the few recruited outside The Association's family of organizations. You'll see why we made an exception in her case.

Before she joined The Association Miranda was manager of consumer banking for a regional bank in the Southeast. She was butting heads with Jason, a peer and manager of commercial lending. Both were vying for the attention of a senior vice president to fund their departments for the forthcoming calendar year. It was annual budgeting time and the usual infighting erupted among peers to grab their share of the money.

Miranda picks up the story[19]:

"The coming year promised to be a doozy. The sub-prime mess had just broke, resulting in a whopping write-off against the bank's earnings. Money was tight and I knew I would have to fight for every dollar in next year's budget.

Remember the old saying 'The squeaky wheel gets the grease?' The managers who holler the loudest and tack on an additional ten percent they don't need seem to get more budgeted dollars than managers who are honest and realistic[20].

Jason, the guy I was competing against for budget resources, was a master at hollering to get what he wanted, and to hell with everybody else. Not that I was any shrinking violet myself. I could holler loud when I had to.

But this year, Jason wasn't hollering. If anything he was guarded, keeping a low profile. This was not the Jason I knew. He was acting as if he had a lock on the budget and it scared me because that could mean my budget was going to flatline or get cut.

One of Jason's lieutenants was Susan, a lady who started with me the same time I did at the bank. I wouldn't exactly call us close friends, but hell, we gals stick together seeing as how we're outnumbered by you men folk. Susan and I routinely swapped nuggets of information that helped us upstage the boys in the bank. All work related, nothing personal or destructive (well, not usually).

Susan knew I was struggling to keep my budget from being cut. She confided that Jason had some 'secret e-mails' he was going to use against me. Well, I don't have to tell you that knocked me for a loop. Those e-mails, whatever they might be, didn't come from me. I never sent an e-mail I would be ashamed to show my mother or my boss, knowing that someday a nasty email message under my name might come back to haunt me.

Susan didn't know who sent the e-mails or what they contained, only that Jason kept them stored on his personal computer. Wherever they came from, I realized I had to get my hands on them and get them fast. But how without breaking the law[21] and exposing myself to criminal prosecution? Please understand, breaking the law to protect myself didn't bother me, only that I couldn't afford to get caught.

I hired a computer nerd, some nineteen-year-old whiz kid who built my home computer for me. I gave him Jason's e-mail address and he used it to locate the Usenet groups[22] Jason frequented. One of those groups Jason belonged to was a bunch of hotshot young male executives who boasted about their female conquests and job successes. You know the type of guys I'm talking about: arrogant puppies who degrade women at every opportunity. Despicable blowhards all.

The group had closed membership, meaning
that applicants had to be approved by the
group's administrator before being granted
access to the members' messages. The nerd
posed as a fellow hotshot and was soon
approved, giving him access to the group's
messages.

Here's what he found: Seems like Jason was
exchanging confidential budgeting information
via e-mail with his counterpart at a competing
bank across town. Those oh-so-clever boys
bragged about their job successes and lorded it
over the women they worked with. Real macho
bullshit. Of course, smarty-pants Jason couldn't
resist bragging to his clubby buddies how he was
going to 'trample me in the dust by revealing
that my operating costs were higher than the
competition's.' He published my costs on his
Usenet group (isn't this unbelievably stupid?),
comparing them with same function at his
buddy's bank, which his asshole buddy was only
too happy to provide seeing as how his costs
were lower than mine. These boys were so cocky
it damaged their brains. Even half-smart
dummies would realize their jobs were on the
line if management in either of the banks found
out they were revealing confidential
information.

According to Jason, my function was fifteen
percent more costly than the same function at
his buddy's bank. A real shocker I knew would

be difficult to explain to my boss. When I told Susan, she said that Jason was going to claim that information was something he overheard at a bankers' association meeting.

Obviously, Jason had no intention of disclosing his cozy quid pro quo arrangement with his buddy from the other bank . . . so I did it for him. I sent our boss, the senior vice president, anonymous copies of Jason's messages from his Usenet group, and that as they say was the beginning of the end for Jason. The asshole was fired forthwith as was his buddy cross-town.

Had I not formed a covert alliance with Susan, and had I not spied on Jason, it would have been me cashing unemployment checks. As it was my budget was slashed fifteen percent, and that hurt, but it sure beat getting canned. And as a big, big bonus I got rid of my chief competitor at the bank."

After hearing this story I wasn't surprised that Miranda came out on top. Proving it never pays to underestimate an adversary, and it's just plain dumb to believe that a woman is less capable than a man. Worse, it's utter stupidity for any male to disrespect a woman's business acumen just because she's a woman. Score one for a low key but highly intelligent and effective corporate player with a great future as a management recruit for The Association.

Strategies from Section Nine

1. Even the most cursory study of the ascendancy of corporate leaders reveals the necessity of basing decisions on reliable information. In military and CIA terms, it's called intelligence, but it's the same thing. Those in the know are those who succeed. Information is king, inside information a kingdom. The route to the executive suite is paved with damaging information you can use against your adversaries and secret information you can use to spot opportunities.

2. Without privileged information about your bosses, peers and subordinates, you're going to make mistakes, one of them possibly a fatal mistake. You simply cannot flourish in Corporate America making too many mistakes or without finding suckers to take the blame.

3. You must get information any way you can. Whatever it takes and whatever you have to do. In any and every way possible. Spying is in, The Golden Rule is out. Need I remind you that management recruits naïve enough to accept the fallacy of The Golden Rule do not make it to the top. Hopefully, we have screened out the foolishly idealistic among you. Not that we expect to find that characteristic from candidates with your background in organized crime. But you never know.

4. A test of your resourcefulness will be how you dig up the information you need and if you get it in a timely

manner. Information that comes to you too late to use is information that's obsolete. It's as useless as yesterday's Drudge Report or Huffington Post online.

5. Remember, in Corporate America legalities are paid homage to in public but circumvented in private. Just as long as players don't get caught, there are no limiting rules. And that's the catch. Don't get caught or your corporate career is blemished, and probably over.

SECTION TEN

The Association's Sixth
Management Commandment

You will remain on guard for attacks from any
and all quarters, especially from peers, and
severely punish those who attack you

The guileless belief that fellow employees are friends in a common pursuit is the hallmark of the novice or the innocent. More often than not, such unenlightened employees turn the other cheek when under attack in the mistaken belief that responding to aggression is to invite more aggression (when in fact the opposite is true). Other employees, although more pragmatic, may not be temperamentally suited for corporate combat and shy away from it. In both instances, unwilling combatants are cannon fodder for the smart corporate player who understands power and how to exercise it.

The smart corporate player intuitively understands the fierce competitive nature of the marketplace. He knows that failure to acknowledge the bellicose tendencies of human nature is a weakness inviting aggression by unforgiving adversaries.

Remember the lawman of the Old West? Here was somebody who never gave the bad guys a second chance. He knew if he did, it would be interpreted as fragility, an open invitation to every gunman within shouting distance to kill or maim him and take over his town. That lonely and courageous lawman understood The Association's Sixth Management Commandment. It was his code; he lived by it or died.

The same code pervades today in the business world. Sure, it's no longer a matter of life or death (although the stress it produces can result in physical damage), but it is a matter of who succeeds and who fails in Corporate America. Indeed, Corporate America is the modern-day equivalent of the Old West, with figurative gunslingers provoking confrontations to exercise power and expand the venue of their authority.

The simple unadorned truth is that you must remain on guard against assaults on your position. It's going to happen; count on it. As you rise in the organization you can expect more frequent, more underhanded and more ferocious attacks because the stakes are higher. You simply cannot allow adversaries to attack you and walk away unscathed. If you do you will be trampled in the dust.

You, of all newly minted corporate employees, should understand this. You come from a crime background where challenges to your authority occur every day. You know that failure to respond aggressively and in a timely fashion will erode your authority . . . if not get you killed. In Corporate America failure to defend your territory is no different. You may walk away with your life intact, but your career will be damaged, possibly beyond repair.

Example

Here's an example from the early career of a corporate player who went on to become CEO of a large automotive supplier. In his own words:

> "I was twenty-seven and recently hired as quality control night shift manager in an automotive assembly plant of a prominent car company. The company, at that time in the late seventies, was attempting to change its reputation of focusing on production at the

expense of quality. The company realized that to effectively compete with the newly emerging threat of high quality Japanese imports, American car quality would have to radically improve.

During my first few days on the job I met Big Bill Cannon[23], the plant's night shift production honcho. Despite a reputation for having run over and ruined the careers of many quality managers in his fifteen years with the company, Big Bill appeared at first blush to be a reasonable, even a personable, guy. I was relieved. Maybe he wasn't such an ogre, after all.

That warm, cuddly feeling was brutally demolished during my first night as second shift quality manager. I knew I was in for it when, at 7:00 p.m., long after the brass cleared the front office and headed for the nearest gin mill, Big Bill had one of his supervisors order me "to git my ass raght fast up to Big Bill's office."

With trepidation approaching alarm, I knocked timidly at his office door, and a deep, intimidating voice boomed, "Come in." I entered slowly to find all of Big Bill's massive 6'6", 280-pound ex-football player frame standing tall, an intimidating presence made even more menacing when he walked up to within inches of me, invading my space.

'Sit down,' he commanded. His face was contorted into a menacing scowl. I sat down obediently.

Big Bill stood there and glared at me, and I mean glared. His eyes locked onto mine in an almost laughable and Neanderthal attempt to intimidate me. He didn't speak, just glared. But it wasn't laughable. What I didn't need was a confrontation on the very first day of my new job.

I wanted to be conciliatory yet I couldn't allow Big Bill's clumsy attempt at domination pass. I instinctively realized that if he got the better of me during my first night on the job I'd lose authority and he'd run me out of the plant as he had so many other quality managers in the past.

What I did was break eye contact and rise and leave his office. 'Where the hell you going?' he bellowed after me. I didn't reply, nor did I stop or look back. I knew what had to be done, and I was going to do it despite an all-consuming fear. I had no choice. Not if I intended to protect the most precious commodity a quality manager must have to survive in the production-oriented environment of the assembly line: his balls.

I marched down the plant's main aisle until I reached the Paint Department and chewed out every quality inspector on the paint line, berating each for not rejecting what would, on any other occasion, be considered minor paint quality flaws.

For those of you unfamiliar with car quality paint standards, they're highly subjective and open to interpretation. It's all as inspectors see it, and they try to judge paint quality with car buyers' eyes.

But not that night. I got after them so much they immediately tightened their standards. Within minutes I had all but choked-off production. Gaps appeared in the assembly line between the Paint Department and the Trim Department (the next department on the assembly line) as swarms of repairmen frantically attempted to correct paint defects and keep cars flowing along the line. Production supervisors screamed at me. I ignored them.

Into this melee of fun and frolic rode an enraged Big Bill Cannon, swooping down upon the Paint department in his electric buggy, his face fire engine red, the cords on his thick neck swollen.

'Fuck you think you're doing?[24]' he demanded to know, standing inches from me, threatening me with a ferocious scowl, his ham-sized fists clenched.

That didn't stop me from saying, 'Your paint quality sucks. I'm not letting it go by.' I was brave on the outside, cowering on the inside, and I was convinced Big Bill saw through me.

'Goddammit, you're rejecting those cars for shit reasons. You don't know your ass from your elbow.'

'Those cars gotta be repaired,' I said. 'Their quality is unacceptable.'

By now supervisors and workers were milling around, gawking at the confrontation. Some snickered, no doubt relishing the opportunity to watch yet another quality sheep fed to the lions.

Somehow I held my ground. Although it was apparent to even the most unobservant I was ready to shit my pants, I stubbornly refused to back down. By then, Big Bill had worked himself into a frenzy. He shouted so much at me he stumbled over words; his fists flailed impotently in the air. He wanted nothing less than to beat the living shit out of me right then and there, but he realized, as did I, that the minute he laid hands on me he was toast. Finally, he spun around and rushed to his buggy, plopped down in it and jabbed a finger at me. 'You're in deep shit now, fellah. I'm calling Jake (the plant manager) and you're fucking history.' With those words echoing after him, he stormed down the aisle towards the main office.

My spirits plunged lower than a snake's belly. I just knew my career was about to come to a screeching halt. Yet, somehow, I managed to calm the inspectors and soon they returned to applying their usual good-sense quality standards.

The end of the shift came and went at 11:00 p.m. I left for home, convinced that I would be called into the plant manager's office the following day and told to pack my bags. Needless to say, I didn't sleep at all that night.

The next afternoon when I reported for my shift I was surprised when nobody said a word to me, other than my boss, who had read the paint quality report and asked what went wrong with the system. He told me that Jake raised hell because Big Bill missed his production quota last night, but he didn't say why. Apparently neither my boss, nor anybody else in the front office, got wind of the previous night's confrontation. I made up some phony story to satisfy my boss's curiosity and headed toward the plant. At the corner of the chassis line (the last operation on the assembly line), I turned and ran smack into Big Bill Cannon. As I started to move past him, he turned and honored me with a wide smile, said hello in a pleasantly modulated voice, a stark contrast to the last night's screams and rants. I walked by in a daze. What the hell?

As I later figured out, Big Bill couldn't afford to openly kiss off car quality. That would have brought down the wrath of God in the form of the plant manager upon him. His foolhardy challenge and my unexpected response caused production to drop twelve percent for his shift.

That's the kiss of death for a car plant production manager. A few of those and he'd be history and Big Bill knew it. He now understood I wouldn't let him get away with his puppy shit war of nerves.

In effect I had called his bluff. In the wake of our confrontation Big Bill's standing took a nosedive. His people no longer considered him invulnerable. A quality nerd, of all people, humiliated him and caused him to lose face among the production workers and line supervisors. He lost that almost magic aura of invincibility that enveloped him. My power expanded as his contracted. It became increasingly difficult for Big Bill to meet the company's demanding production schedule. When a year later I was promoted to plant quality manager, Big Bill was no longer around to congratulate me. He had been transferred to another assembly plant."

Strategies from Section Ten

1. Here's a maxim of corporate life that is the same for organized crime: You cannot ever give any indication of weakness or uncertainty even when you're temporarily unsure of a course of action. Nor can you back down from a challenge. Do so and bosses, peers and subordinates will lose respect for you. Displays of weakness are an open invitation for ambitious peers to drive a figurative stake in your heart. You must strike hard and without mercy at those who stand in your way, those who challenge your authority and those who mean you harm.

2. Never let your guard down. Never. Keep in mind that during your journey to the top ranks of Corporate America, you will be challenged every step of the way by ambitious peers eager to grab the golden ring, to snatch it from your grasp at any expense. This is an unalterable fact of corporate life. To paraphrase a great saying by Thomas Jefferson, "the price of corporate success is eternal vigilance.[25]"

3. Do not underestimate the shrewdness of your adversaries. They'll seldom attack you openly but they will attack you. And they'll be clever about how they do it. Assume frequent back door or flanking attacks designed to catch you off-guard. You may not even be aware of their unfriendly intentions until the blade is slipping between your ribs, and by then it's too late. A test of your skill and resourcefulness will be how well prepared you are to identify threats looming on the horizon and how quickly you're able

to counter the thrusts of knife artists engaged in corporate combat and emerge victorious.

4. Answer back door or flanking attacks with back door and flanking attacks of your own. Don't hesitate to play dirty. The dirtier you play, the dirtier the scheme you concoct to defeat adversaries, the more you'll scare off enemies. Like your corporate brethren, disguise your actions with a smile and a handshake. Overt action will only get you in trouble.

SECTION ELEVEN

The Association's Seventh
Management Commandment

You will never fail to meet and exceed a goal,
regardless of how many bodies fall, as long as
one of those bodies is not your own

Just about everybody in Corporate America understands that achieving goals is the cornerstone of success, both for employees and their companies. Failure to fulfill planned goals such as sales, profits, inventory levels, quality, customer service and a dozen or so related measures can seriously hobble company performance and reduce the wages and salaries of employees.

But not everybody agrees on where to draw the line; where the pursuit of objectives becomes so focused and intense that it damages employee welfare. Three schools of thought prevail:

The first, composed of corporate innocents, places people over goals. Its proponents are disgusted when corporate players subvert the process for their own benefit and step on fellow employees for personal gain. Such corporate innocents seldom achieve executive status and often are displaced by more ambitious and calculating managers, yet their righteous perspective rarely changes. They are commonly referred to as purists.

The second, a type of shifty corporate player, has little or no regard for employee welfare but pretends he does. He sniffs out the level of improvement that satisfies his boss, say a five percent hike in productivity, and focuses on achieving it, even when he could produce improvements of fifteen percent. Why bust your ass, his thinking goes, when the boss will accept five percent and pat you on the back for it? Banking the other ten percent just makes it easier the next two years and keeps the shifty corporate player in high regard.

Finally, we are left with the brand of aggressive corporate player that you must be if you intend to achieve early and continuing corporate success.

The aggressive corporate player is on a fast track. He does not accept the notion of slow and steady improvements like his counterpart, the shifty corporate player, nor does he have the restrictive scruples of the corporate innocent. If, for example, he is manager of a unit with one-hundred people and knows he could get the same amount of work out with eighty employees, the other twenty will get chopped fast. If his bosses give the command for twenty layoffs, he will fire twenty-five. This player always stays ahead of the curve; he invariably exceeds top management's expectations. His aim is to make a name for himself and move up quickly in the organization. Dramatic operating improvements enhance his reputation as a doer.

Such fast-track corporate players will do whatever is necessary to advance their careers. Moral judgments, such as those that dominate the perspective of purists, do not play a role. As for the shifty corporate player, the difference between him and the aggressive corporate player is one of pace. One moves slower than the other, but both are similarly ruthless. Their every action is geared to climbing the corporate pyramid no matter how many bodies fall, as long as they're not included in the body count. The aggressive corporate player reaches the top faster, much faster, because at heart the shifty corporate player does not have the heart for the game; his approach is conservative and exceedingly cautious. The aggressive corporate player understands the importance of speedy and prodigious results. That's what counts because that's what top management says that counts.

Examples

The president of a large branded luggage company told me this story:

> "The salesman for our Chicago district was retiring after thirty years of service, the last twenty of it in Chicago. This guy was one of our highest producing salespeople in the company. Not the managerial type, but great with customers. He knew how to schmooze better than most in the business and ground out his numbers every month without fail. Never once missed a sales quota that I know of. An amazing performance greatly admired throughout the company.
>
> The big concern was who to replace him with. The fear was that his replacement would not be able to maintain the same high levels of sales as the much respected retiree. Management thought long and hard about it and decided to put a fresh company face in the slot, so they hired a bright, aggressive kid right out of graduate school.
>
> Guess what happened? First month on the job the kid matched the old pro's quota. Second month he doubled it. Management thought it must be some fluke so they sent a home office

sales expert to the field to find out. The expert came away impressed with the kid. Everybody at company headquarters was puzzled. Nobody expected the surge to continue.

Third month, the kid, hitting his stride, almost triples the old pro's quota, and from there on out the numbers keep rolling in. By the end of the kid's first year on the job he was cruising along at sales levels about two-and-one-half times what the old pro produced.

What management finally realized was that the old pro wasn't as much an old pro as everybody gave him credit for. Somehow, early in his Chicago gig, he convinced upper sales management that his numbers were better than anybody else could produce, and everybody bought into it, from sales management to upper management. From then on, the old pro's performance earned him spectacular bonuses every year. The old guy fooled the entire company for many years and it took a freshman salesman to expose it.

As you would expect, the kid earned a fast promotion to district sales manager, responsible for Ohio and Illinois. Can you guess what happened the year following his promotion? I can see you nodding your head and smiling. Yeah, the kid did it again. The sales levels for his district increased forty percent over the first year-and-a-half. Another promotion and he's now regional sales manager for the entire territory west of the Mississippi. Same story. Sales exploded.

Besides being a natural salesman, the kid was a whiz at designing new systems to run his area with significant fewer salespeople, customer service representatives and administrative employees. That further juiced up profits. Out went any employee who wasn't needed, and believe me, they went out fast. In common vernacular, the bodies fell by the dozens and the lines at local unemployment offices swelled. The kid was that good. Sure, he gained a reputation as a ruthless cost cutter, and wasn't top management secretly delighted by it. Everybody in the executive suite lay claim to being the one responsible for bringing the kid on board."

At this stage of his story, the president smiled and asked me what he thought happened to the kid? I politely told him I didn't know but would sure like to find out.

"Well, you're looking at him. I was that kid and I became the youngest president of the company. Surprised?"

Not in the slightest.

Here's another example that corroborates the value of The Association's Seventh Career Commandment as told to me by the retired chairman and CEO of one of the country's better management consulting companies:

"Many years ago I was a consultant specializing in a cost reduction procedure called short-interval scheduling, a system used to cut substantial numbers of employees from company payrolls. A system, incidentally, roundly criticized by some executives for being too disruptive on their organizations, but one justified given the excessive number of employees most companies carry on their payrolls.

Our most aggressive supporters, almost zealots, were smart corporate players within the client companies who embraced our consulting efforts to advance their careers. What better way to get recognition than by dramatically reducing headcounts and related payroll costs? These ambitious men and women realized that top company executives who bought the expensive consulting services were closely monitoring progress to make sure they got the biggest bang for their buck. We counted on such support from managers like that because installation of the system and its resulting layoff of employees was a shock to remaining employees and often tended to erode morale.

Frankly, we charged a small fortune. Normally our consulting contract called for fees amounting to one-third of the annualized cost savings our services generated. For example, say we cut one-hundred employees, and the cost of each employee to the company was about $30,000, our fees amounted to a million dollars ($30,000/3 = $10,000 per employee x 100).

The typical number of employees short-interval scheduling allowed us to cut from the payroll ranged from twenty percent to thirty percent, sometimes more. Not unheard of numbers in my former business.

The point is that successful installation of our system helped ambitious managers, most of them in middle management, become overnight stars and those selected by top management for rapid advancement. It takes a lot of courage to implement a system that cuts a third of your costs without affecting output, and only the best and the brightest have what it takes."

Here's the lesson for Association management recruits: Chances are you're going to be running operations with hundreds, and someday thousands, of employees. If you're resourceful enough to latch onto a system like short-interval scheduling and cut payroll costs thirty percent you'll shine not only in top management's eyes but also in the eyes of employees remaining on the payroll. Why? Because you're going to sell those employees on the fact that if their company doesn't reduce headcounts, the entire function or entire company will be shipped to India or China or Mexico or Costa Rica and everybody will lose their jobs.

Installing a dramatic new program like the one described is an opportunity to leap over your competitors and achieve early executive status. But there's a downside risk. Installation of the cost reduction technique must be successful or your career could stall. These programs cost a lot of money and payback is essential.

Strategies from Section Eleven

1. During your corporate career you will be looked upon as a rising star if you know how to get more work done with fewer employees. In corporate parlance, this means cutting headcounts to the bone. Top management loves a cost cutter and lavishes him or her with praise, money and promotions. It's fast track city for those able to meet the demands.

2. The same goes for sales. The stars shine brightly for those who know how to generate new sales while cutting manufacturing and sales support costs. Those adept at developing new products and markets on the cheap, gaining new customers without spending a fortune on development costs, persuading existing customers to order more . . . well, those men and women will climb the corporate ladder at mach speed. Everybody loves a winner.

3. Be careful that any cost reduction effort is successful and does not falter. If it doesn't payback as predicted (remember in Corporate America everything you do is measured by cost vs. benefits), all those pats on the back and all those smiles from the executive suite will evaporate faster than a drop of water on a hot frying pan. Nobody likes a loser, especially the guys and gals on the top floor.

4. Keep in mind that one "aw shit" cancels a hundred "atta boys." You can have a dozen successful quarters but slip in the next quarter and smiles turn to frowns. If the following quarter is as bad as the one before it,

you're in - as the poet says - deep shit territory. You simply can't allow this to happen to you. That first slip is a warning: Do whatever necessary to get back on track regardless of what it takes or how many employees you must sacrifice.

5. Any cost reduction program involving the layoff of significant numbers of employees is frequently successful at first, then loses steam over time. This is because enthusiastic managers hungry to make a name for themselves cut too many employees. The sheer momentum of the new program will carry the day until fatigue sets in. That's why it's so important to keep a few extra employees on the payroll when you make your cuts. After all, you'll be just as well respected by top management for a twenty-seven percent reduction in your payroll costs instead of a thirty percent reduction. Incidentally, this is not the same play as the shifty corporate manager described previously. That guy was dealing in five percent cuts. You've got the balls to work in the twenty-five to thirty percent range.

6. If you are in the position to take over a function from a manager whose performance was poor or at best marginally acceptable, you'll have an splendid opportunity to excel. Where problems exist opportunities abound. What the guy before you failed to do you may conquer with ease. Stay in tune to what's going on in your company and you'll soon learn where the problems and opportunities are. When an opening occurs you'll know if it's best for you. Then strike and start cutting costs.

SECTION TWELVE

The Association's Eighth Management Commandment

You will, through furtive means, make both
your peers' mistakes and your personal
successes known to top management

Job etiquette requires that you should never go over your boss' head without his permission. Particularly if you're trying to blow your own horn or slip it to a job adversary. Most corporate employees adhere to this rule either because they're foolish enough to believe it or because they're afraid of the consequences should they elect to do so.

This traditional approach poses several problems for corporate players on the make. First, you won't know what top management thinks of you or other comers. If you and an adversary lock horns in a battle for promotion it's imperative that you find out where you stand with the people who count. Otherwise, you're casting your fate to the winds. Your adversary could get to top management first and whisper some ungodly and untrue rumors about you that could damage your career. Of course, it's perfectly acceptable - let me change that, it's crucial - that you get there first and ravage your adversary's reputation instead. In a gentlemanly manner, of course, such that it appears you have your adversary's well being in mind ("Poor Jeff, he means well, but frankly he's struggling with this assignment. He needs help."). The Association's corollary to its eighth management commandment says it best: Always Keep in Mind It's Not What You Know, Not Even Necessarily Whom You Know, But Who Screws Whom First That Separates Winners from Losers.

Sure, you recognize what a wonderful job you're doing, and you know that your adversary has flubbed assignments, but does the brass have that same information? Suppose your boss favors your adversary and is leaning toward selecting him for a promotion. Do you think, under those circumstances, he's going to expose your adversary's flaws to top management? You know he isn't. Leaving you sucking hind tit.

Even should your boss favor you, can you be sure your adversary doesn't have a rabbi in high places advocating his promotion? If so, do you think your boss is going to cross swords with a powerful rabbi to protect you? Get the picture?

The bottom line is that you must somehow gain access to the right people in top management to plant favorable information about you and unfavorable information about your adversaries.

The smart corporate player does not leave anything to chance when it concerns his career. He finds ways to make sure his reputation is intact among the people who count and his adversary's reputations in tatters. For a good example of how yours' truly schmoozed a rabbi read the example in Section Two of this handbook. For another, see the example described below showing how a middle manager gained the confidence of his company's chairman.

The smart corporate player understands that making his successes known to top management, as well as his adversary's mistakes, is a delicate affair where sensitivity counts. This is not the arena for bare knuckles brawling. It's more a matter of afternoon tea at the Hamptons. Finesse, ingenuity, guile and manipulation are key characteristics that define successful corporate players.

Smart corporate players never go over their bosses' heads with problems, just imaginative solutions that capture the attention of top floor policymakers. They realize that executives do not want to be burdened with somebody else's problems. That's the key to corporate oblivion.

Smart corporate players also intuitively realize that jumping over their bosses' heads carries risks. If the attempts fail, they'll be branded as ass kissers and their careers shattered. Be cautious and plan your moves accordingly.

Examples

Here's a nasty tactic that will sink your adversary faster than a torpedo sinks a rowboat. In this case the victim told me his story.

> "At the time I had been hired as back office manager for a flourishing Wall Street brokerage firm. The expectation was that I would work this job for about six months and then get promoted to vice president over the entire operation, a new position. Jerry, a peer and the brokerage's financial controller for back office operations made a lot of time available to help me during my first weeks on the job. We became fast friends, not only at work but socially as well. We were both married and lived close by in New Jersey, and the four of us went out to dinner just about every weekend.

About five months into the job Jerry and I were working together to implement a new computer-driven loss control system to reduce the number of lost and misplaced stock certificates. I was in charge of the project since in brokerage firms back office operation management was king and staff services such as Jerry's were viewed as support. As it should be.

The project was going quite well and ahead of schedule. Jerry suggested that I write a memo to be widely distributed among the company's senior staff, advocating the adoption of the same loss control system for the company's San Francisco and Chicago affiliate offices. I followed his suggestion and wrote the memo and had it widely distributed.

About a week later I was sitting in my office and was shocked to receive the CEO's copy of my memo with some pretty direct and nasty comments in black ink scribbled across the memo. Seems the top honcho believed it doesn't pay to rush into anything new involving computer systems, especially when it involves outlying operations and most particularly when it doesn't concern my area of responsibility.

I don't know if you ever had anything you proposed shot down by the CEO of your company, but I can tell you it shook me to the core; it was akin to a slap in the face. I made an appointment to see him, which he granted. He was nice enough during the meeting, but the upshot was that until proven over time, the computer-driven loss control system would be confined to New York.

It was clear that by writing and widely circulating the memo I had stepped into a deep pile of shit. The memo my good buddy Jerry advised me to send.

Jerry, the cutthroat son-of-a-bitch, set me up, and like a donkey I followed his advice. What I didn't know, and should have, was that Jerry was watching out for Jerry, and he wanted to sabotage my efforts so he could shine by comparison. No doubt he told the company CEO that he advised me to take it slow, but I was too headstrong to listen to him.

I plead guilty to jumping ahead without first thinking out why Jerry was so gung ho and what he had to gain. My rush to get the job done is both a blessing and an Achilles heel. Jerry figured me out correctly and he couldn't have found a better way to make me look bad. The sneaky prick. I'm still fuming even though this happened a few years ago. But I guess you can see that, can't you?

As you can imagine I was persona non grata after that. I had no choice but to leave the company as soon as I found a comparable job elsewhere."

Here's a another example: When I was in middle management and competing for my first vice-presidency at International MacroSystems I was in hot competition with Byron, another middle manager.

In Corporate America, as you'll soon discover, head-knocking competition among peers is customary and expected (figuratively speaking, of course). Most top executives deliberately set one manager against the other in the expectation that fierce competition will bring out the best in them. Well, it brings out the best, all right. The best cutthroat tactics, the best aggressive posturing, the best underhanded and nasty stratagems, the best game playing and last but certainly not least the most skillful ass kissers. That's the nature of corporate competition and frankly, it's a practice that has its merits. I have set subordinates against other subordinates many times during my corporate career, but not in the unrealistic belief that it fosters competition; that's nonsense. I do it to see which candidate is tougher, more resilient and best able to handle the combat. And sometimes, knowing which candidate is best suited for corporate combat, it's a way to force the weaker candidate out of the picture. Leaving behind a defeated job adversary is comparable to poisoning the well. He'll try to make his former adversary and now boss look foolish, and that helps nobody. Not the company, certainly not the successful adversary and not the defeated competitor. The time he spends trying to bring somebody down could be better used in a new job rebuilding his reputation through positive contributions.

My adversary Byron had a weak spot. He flew off the handle on occasion when subordinates disappointed him and berated them in front of other employees. A big no no in Corporate America where even the smallest public display of emotion is frowned upon. I also happened to know that Byron had confined his rants and raves to employees in his department: programmers, system analysts, clerks and other lower level employees. Top management was unaware of his tantrums. Byron presented a calmer face to his bosses.

Hmmm. Loaded with possibilities, wasn't it?

A software engineer in Byron's organization whom I befriended was leaving the company and working his notice. I asked him if he wouldn't mind provoking Byron. He enthusiastically rubbed his hands together and agreed. The poor guy had suffered through several tongue lashings from Byron and he had no love for him, to put it mildly.

I arranged to take an important customer through the company's operations, accompanied by my boss's boss, a senior vice president of the company. At the same time we passed through Byron's area, the software engineer who owed me a favor provoked Byron, who predictably flew into a rage. Unfortunately for Byron both the customer and my boss' boss witnessed this ugly demonstration. That, as you can guess, was the end of Lord Byron's dreams of advancement in International MacroSystems. Now, how in the world did I know that Byron would behave like an uncontrolled ape at exactly the right moment? My, my, the wonders of the world will never cease.

Strategies from Section Twelve

1. Study your adversaries, their strengths and weaknesses. You will soon learn their vulnerabilities. Sometimes they're well hidden. Your responsibility is to expose them any way you can. Everybody has an Achilles' heel; many have several. Find them through observing your adversary in action. Learn about his past. Learn what subordinates and peers say about him. Sooner or later you will uncover his weak spots. Then decide how to expose him in such a way that top management hears about his fatal flaws.

2. Strike hard and strike fast when exposing your adversaries' failures, but be especially careful to hide your identity. Top management does not publicly award whistleblowers or those it considers bootlickers. But don't kid yourself: Executives, like anybody else in management, want to know who is succeeding and who is fucking up. Oftentimes that knowledge is screened from them by subordinate managers with their own agendas. Your duty is to supply the real skinny to those who make command decisions.

3. That brings up the next point. You must be insightful enough to understand where your strengths and weaknesses lie, with the obvious corollary that you should build on your strengths and hide your weaknesses. If, for example, you are a strong line manager and weak in staff functions, then obviously you want to work in line operations where you stand out. If at some time management assigns you to a staff function, grit your teeth, do your best possible

and get back to a line job as soon as you find an appropriate opening. In the meantime, find somebody in your staff assignment who can help you, somebody who knows the ropes and feels comfortable in staff work. But make no mistake about it, if you stay in a staff capacity too long your job performance may suffer, such that your reputation loses its luster.

4. Find some imaginative way to bring your successes to the attention of top decision makers, those who have the power to advance your career. Simply bragging about your successes may not necessarily do the trick. In fact, it seldom does. It might brand you as a bullshitter. You may have to connive to make top management aware of how truly wonderful you are. This is a perfect time to have somebody else blow your horn. A friend in high places helps. You're smart, you can figure out what to do. Plan carefully and execute relentlessly.

SECTION THIRTEEN

The Association's Ninth Management Commandment

You will find fall guys for your mistakes

The prevailing wisdom among John-Wayne-type corporate warriors is to stand tall and admit your mistakes, take your punishment like a man, resolve to improve your failings and go forth, head held high with grit and determination.

What happy horseshit! Show me such a man or woman in Corporate America - the real Corporate America, not the bogus one described in high-sounding tomes or TV soap operas - and I'll show you a cartoon cutout. That person rarely exists, and when he does he'll be cut to pieces by shrewder competitors who know how to shift the blame for their mistakes to dummies with broad shoulders and empty heads. The Duke may have whipped the West into shape, but his business twin was never devious enough to ride the corridors of Corporate America.

Don't ever get it into your head that you are invulnerable. Nobody, repeat nobody, ever gets through work without making mistakes, a few of them grand enough to sink careers. Granted, alert corporate players - and you want to be counted among them - make few mistakes of the grievous kind that destroy careers. But they do make them, and when they do, they need a fallback position (somebody to blame). That's where fall guys come in.

Back home, if you made too many mistakes you lost not only your job, but possibly your kneecaps. The Mob does not tolerate failure, and once you were declared incompetent by the bosses there was no place for you to go. You were no longer considered capable of working as a "soldier". Sure, it's possible the bosses would have allowed you to work outside the Family, but for how long? You knew too much and you could no longer be trusted. From there it was a short ride to a pair of cement shoes on a boat off the New Jersey shore.

Your only alternative was to hide your mistakes and pin them on some other poor slob. Preferably some slob outside the Family. Either that or suffer the consequences. If you've made it this far through the rigorous selection process The Association uses to select its management recruits, and you're now residing in Corporate America, chances are you've mastered the fine art of blaming others. If not, read on. Your corporate success may well depend on it.

Okay, you're saying, I understand what you're telling me. But where do I find a shill stupid enough to stand in for my mistakes in Corporate America? Good question. Here's a partial list of corporate personalities that should provide some clues:

- Start with the empty-headed John Wayne tall-in-the-saddle type I described in the opening paragraph. The dude will never know what hit him. He'll take months to figure out he's been had and by the time he does his grievance will sound like sour grapes; too late to shift the blame back onto your shoulders.

- Lay the blame on some technical guru involved in a project that sizzled. Technical gurus aren't normally endowed with much political savvy; they're more comfortable solving technological and scientific problems. As such they're perfect fall guys because they're easily blindsided.

- Those unfortunates on top management's shit list are perfect targets. They already have one foot out the door. A nudge provided by you will complete the job and nobody will be the wiser. If those losers bitch about your Machiavellian methods nobody will listen because they've lost all credibility. Just make sure you're not caught in the act of nudging unless you don't mind joining those already on the shit list.

- Get close to an adversary. Become friends, socialize with him. Once he trusts you (silly boy) and opens up about his feelings and especially his failings, you'll be in a position to take advantage of them at the appropriate time. By shifting management's focus to his flaws you'll provide a distraction that removes the focus from your mistake.

- Here's one I'll bet you never thought of: You should always keep one member on your staff whom you can sacrifice when the shit hits the fan. Somebody you identified earlier as disposable; somebody you keep around for the inevitable day when you make a grand faux pas and you're desperately seeking a way to cover your ass. Such a person - cannon fodder, really - is the perfect fall guy. Nasty but effective. Read on to see how.

Examples

The following examples indicate the type of planning that succeeds in establishing an invaluable fall guy. In this first case the example is mine.

Early in my corporate career, when I was about to be promoted to sales and marketing manager for a growing division of my company, my soon-to-be boss offered his opinion of the sales people who would be working for me: the achievers, the slackers, the drifters, that kind of opinionated evaluation. He singled out one non-performer in particular, Norman, a district sales manager whom he thought should have been fired long ago, but my predecessor had kept Norman on in the vain effort to turn him into an acceptable producer.

I spent some time talking to and evaluating Norman and came to the conclusion that he was far from the brightest bulb in the marquee and would never be capable of the twenty-five percent increase in sales I was planning on.

On reflection I decided to keep him around in a low-key sales administrative position he could handle because he had a lot of invaluable product knowledge that would help my district sales managers.

I can see you chuckling to yourself because you already know enough about my scheming mind to realize I had something sinister up my sleeve. Well, chuckle away because you're dead right. I went to bat for Norman and convinced my boss he could handle the administrative function. So I turned Norman loose on the job and he proved my assumption correct. The district sales managers let me know that Norman was a big help.

Of course, I now had tucked away in my organization a potential fall guy. Norman was bright enough to handle his job but not bright enough to figure out why I kept him on and what I was planning for him.

Two years later the shit hit the fan when the economy tanked and our sales dropped enough that my division narrowly missed its sales goal. But in business you better recognize two factors regarding missed goals. First, a miss, regardless of how close, is as good as a mile. Whether it's one percent or twenty percent, the bottom line is that you missed. There are no one percent missed successes.

Second (and this bears repeating) one "aw shit, you missed" cancels one-hundred "atta boys, you made your budgeted sales." In business you are only as good as your current performance. Top management doesn't dwell on past successes, only the current quarter. Like it or not, unfair as it may be, that's an incontrovertible fact of business life.

Which left me, as sales and marketing manager, holding the bag. What to do to save my ass?

You guessed it. I went to my boss, hat in hand, and confessed that we missed our sales quota because Norman failed to provide timely product samples to two key customers, which prompted a delay in their orders. Enough to make my team narrowly miss its quarterly sales goal. Not really true, but who cares? I told my boss he was right all along about Norman and I should have listened to him. That flattered my boss, of course. Nothing like eating a little humble pie when you know the pie tastes good. I assured him that in the next quarter we would easily exceed sales forecasts such that I could make up for this quarter and surge ahead for the year. Of course I later busted my ass to make it happen.

By going to my boss, hat in hand and confessing my failure, I was really doing nothing more than massaging his swollen ego, which he ate up. The bottom line is that I gained stature in my boss' eyes while booting Norman out the door for his "big mistake." Within a matter of weeks I was looking around for another fall guy to plant in my organization.

Here's another example that will knock your socks off. One stormy Friday night I waited in Dallas's DFW International airport to catch a plane home after a full week of wining and dining customers and signing new orders in the Dallas-Ft. Worth area. I stopped off at a bar for a relaxing well-earned martini when the PA system announced that all flights would be delayed for an indefinite time due to violent thunderstorms and high winds. A collective groan emerged from the assembled drinkers. The businessman perched next to me at the bar struck up a conversation and, as the hours passed and our drinking continued, we became chummier and chummier, telling each other stories from work. Neither of us mentioned our names or our companies or anything else of a personal nature. He was traveling home to Chicago and I was returning to the East Coast.[26] That anonymity made for looser tongues because we both knew that chances were we would never run into each other again.

Anyway, here's the story he told me, as I recall it:

"A few years ago I joined the company I work for now, hired in as manufacturing manager for its largest plant. Three years later, the company was in the throes of developing a radically new product line with high sales expectations. By chance I was familiar with it because my former company had developed a similar product. Manufacturing endured so many technical problems the company eventually stopped production and wrote off the loss.

"When I told my boss about the experience he patted my back and told me not to worry. Our product is different, he claimed. His engineers had licked the many frustrating technical problems my former company encountered. Not to worry.

"I knew better, but since my boss, the company's vice president of manufacturing, was, shall we say, bullheaded, he insisted on having it his way.

"His intransigence handed me an unprecedented opportunity. One pain-in-the-ass guy who worked for me, the process engineering manager, was buddy-buddy with my boss. I often found them both with their heads so close together you would have thought they were lovers (maybe they were). This couldn't help but make me wonder how secure my position was. I dug into their relationship and discovered that my boss wanted his process engineering buddy promoted to the manufacturing manager's job but his selection was nixed by top management.

"I realized that the longer the process engineering manager worked for me the more tenuous my position would become. He already was going over my head to appeal decisions I made.

"Well, enough is enough. I talked my boss into promoting his asshole buddy into the job of production manager for the new and experimental product line. He quickly agreed and went so far as to separate that part of the manufacturing organization and have it report directly to him. That way the two buddies wouldn't have me interfering with their cozy relationship, and didn't they love it.

"The new product line fell flat on its ass - as I told my boss it would. The boys upstairs shut down the project in six months and canned both my boss and his great buddy. I kind of helped it along by telling the executive vice president about my previous experience with the product and how I had tried to stop my boss from moving ahead with it. The final nail in the asshole's coffin.

"I'll bet you've already ventured a guess as to how this worked out for yours truly. If you deduced that I'm now the company's new vice president of manufacturing, you would be one-hundred percent spot on and I owe you a drink."

I told him it didn't surprise me in the least and he bought me a martini.

Another Friday night. Another airport bar. Another no-name story. This time I've reconstructed the dialogue as best as I recollect because the can-do, must-do attitude of the guy telling the story is the exact attitude you need to win at the great game of business. This guy understands that ethics and corporate success are diametrically opposed. He realizes that success is based on a willingness to cut throats (figuratively, of course) without hesitation or remorse.

That Friday evening at the airport bar, after a little harmless introductory chit-chat about the weather and last Sunday's NFL games we ingested a couple of martinis and exchanged corporate war stories, again without mentioning names or companies. The conversation loosened up when the guy I was matching drinks with said, "Look, you don't know me and I don't know you. What I'm about to tell you I've never told another person before, the wife included. I don't mind telling you because I don't know who you are or anything else about you, and you know absolutely nothing about my identity, and after tonight I don't plan on seeing you again." He sighed. "It's great to let my hair down, particularly with somebody like you who I sense is exactly like me."

I asked him how we compare.

"Cold-hearted, focused on goals to the exclusion of anything else, people included."
I chuckled. His intuition was right on the mark. It takes a schemer to recognize a schemer.

If anybody at work even suspected the kind of guy I am I'd be..." His voice trailed off and he ran a finger across his throat. After a few moments of staring at his drink, he said, "There's a guy who works for me, an MBA[27], fairly high level, real bright, a possible opponent for promotion. Not everybody can control his aggressive behavior, but I can and I do. For the sake of our discussion let's call him Harvey. Anyway, purely by accident I found out from a headhunter that Harvey was shopping his resume around. Not that he was ready to bolt, mind you, just keeping his fingers in the water.

Never hurts to know what opportunities are available. I don't blame Harvey for keeping abreast of the market. I do it myself but I'm more cautious than Harvey. I sure as hell don't send out resumes, but I do talk with headhunters and friends who are aware of open jobs in the marketplace. I'm careful not to leave a paper trail.

The headhunter I mentioned owed me. I had given him a lot of work finding job candidates for our company and now it paid off. To stay on my good side he let me see a copy of Harvey's resume. I now had Harvey by the short hairs, and best of all worlds, he didn't know it.

To make a long story short, I was in charge of a project that was encountering some unexpected turbulence, to borrow a phrase from the airlines. Costs were running unexpectedly high and over budget. Predictably, top management was looking for either a quick fix or a way out. Should the project fail, there was going to be a scapegoat. Somebody in the project management team, probably me, was going to get booted out along with the project itself if I didn't come up with a solution pronto. Nobody in the executive suite was going to take the blame; that's how it always is.

I knew how I could rescue the project but I needed the wholehearted support of my staff to get it done. Mr. Bright Guy Harvey was not going all out and I knew it. He was hedging his bets, counting on me falling flat on my ass and guess who would be in position to take over my job. Or so Harvey thought.

Well, I provided the fall guy that the top floor demanded. I had my headhunter buddy surreptitiously email Harvey's resume to about a dozen companies, three of them competitors, two of them subsidiaries of the company we both worked for. The human resources guys in our subsidiaries predictably forwarded Harvey's resume to our human resource guy who made a point to let me know that Harvey was looking elsewhere for employment.

Perfect. I had my opening. I confessed that Harvey was not paying attention to his job such that costs in his section were spiraling out of control. They weren't but since Harvey's costs were buried in with the costs of other section leaders my boss wouldn't know that. My ploy worked. My boss and I, with the concurrence of the human resources director, reached a decision to fire Harvey. It was approved by a senior vice president and out Harvey went. The guys upstairs had their fall guy (and so did I) and my reputation remained unblemished. Of course I had to fix things fast, but that's what I'm famous for. I did that in double time and enhanced my reputation with top management."

I couldn't have done it better, myself. You can learn from this story. Be prepared to offer up a sacrificial lamb. Just make sure you're not skewering yourself in the process.

Strategies from Section Thirteen

1. It's important to realize that sooner or later you're going to make a meaningful mistake. Meaningful in the sense that its consequences could damage your career, as opposed to minor mistakes that will not alter your upward career path. We all make the latter kind of mistakes, but it's the former kind you must prepare for.

2. Getting out from under takes careful thought. For that reason it's critical that whatever project you're assigned to, you must clearly identify a potential fall guy, man or woman, and plan how to shift responsibility to that person. The last thing you want is top management blaming you for the resulting substandard performance. Those words "substandard performance" cannot ever become recorded in your personnel jacket, or your future is as bright as a homeless person's. As I've mentioned repeatedly, The Association does not accept failure. You already know that and understand the consequences of not succeeding.

3. Use your job smarts and political savvy to assure that top management - those who hold your future in their hands - will not suspect you're behind the fall guy's setup. An illustrative example is the manufacturing manager's story described above.

4. It's just as important to realize you can't go to the well too often. A series of mistakes, albeit with fall guys in place, may alert somebody in the executive

suite to your possible involvement, thereby sealing your fate both with your company and The Association. With a bit of luck you will make only one, at most two, grievous career errors in your rise to the top. More than that may expose you and place your career in jeopardy. You have been screened carefully to assure your eventual ascendancy to the top position in your company, but that doesn't mean you can ever let your guard down.

SECTION FOURTEEN

The Association's Tenth
Management Commandment

You will move through middle management
as quickly as possible, for it is the most
dangerous organizational level of all

Middle management is a swamp from which few aspiring managers escape. It is the classical management trap where first-line supervisors and technical people ascend to their level of incompetence and stall out. The best that most middle managers can hope for is to hold onto their jobs in middle management until retirement. Many are demoted or leave for other companies. Others are shuffled sideways from one middle management position to the next until the day company executives realizes they can replace them with aspiring employees making less money. A very few ascend to upper management.

Middle managers are caught between the often divergent needs of executives responsible for setting policy and front-line supervisors responsible for results on the firing line. For example, executives might determine a need to cut costs ten percent to maintain gross profit levels. They ask middle managers to examine their organizations and see where they can make cuts. Ten percent is feasible for many of the operating departments, but there are always instances where that high a cut might slice away muscle instead of fat at the bottom of the organization. Most middle managers will resist cutting costs when first-line supervisors dig in their heels and yell foul. Typically, what happens then is a frustrated top management team issues a decree to cut costs across-the-board. This sequence of events presents you with an opportunity to make a name for yourself. Now is the time to ride in on your white horse and make the cost cuts in your area of responsibility. Your peers will look uncooperative claiming they're unable to follow your lead. That's exactly what you want.

Why aren't more middle managers responsive to the needs of their companies? Because, despite assertions to the contrary, they have lax views on the capabilities of their supervisors and workers, making them reluctant (actually, afraid) to accept the challenge of cutting costs. Other, shrewder, middle managers load their fiefdoms with excessive numbers of employees in the mistaken assumption that sheer size is equivalent to power, when in fact the opposite is true. Add to that the opposition of front-line supervisors - those people on the firing line directly responsible for getting out high quality work on time and within budget - and you can now understand the key weakness in middle management. But it's the middle managers, whom the top floor looks to when sticky issues such as this emerge. Under such circumstances executives, by necessity, consider slashing middle management ranks, if for nothing more than to replace inflexible middle managers with new blood more amenable to executive mandates.

Another hazard: Middle managers in staff functions are especially vulnerable. Middle managers in line operations such as sales and production are less likely to get cut as opposed to middle managers in support functions such as marketing, advertising, engineering, maintenance and accounting where cuts do not immediately affect sales and production numbers. Still, they're all vulnerable to one degree or another.

Here's another scary scenario. Once you ascend to middle management ranks, executives might consider you too valuable to promote. This happens repeatedly, principally when managers possess technical skills that are hard to replace. For example, if you were promoted into the position of manager of product engineering in a department whose work record was considered inferior, and you turned the operation around such that the department was now exceeding expectations, top management might be reluctant to promote you, concerned that there's nobody in sight who could perform as well as you in that function. The obvious way to avoid this trap is to develop a second-in-command whose skills are readily apparent to both you and your bosses (but only if you are sure other, higher, opportunities await you in the company. Otherwise, the top floor gang might consider you replaceable.)

You must move quickly through middle management ranks, the quicksand of careers, because the more time you spend there, the more likely you are to get stuck there. And that is not where The Association wants you. Your objective is to advance as rapidly as possible through middle management ranks regardless of the pitfalls you encounter, regardless of the people you must step on or over, regardless of the tactics you must employ. In your budding career in Corporate America, remember that the moment you are promoted to middle manager is the exact moment you must plan to escape it.

What steps must you take to assure a rapid ascent through middle management?

- Groom a successor. As I just said, don't get caught in the trap of being indispensable. Just make sure your potential successor doesn't become so attractive a candidate that it's a temptation to replace you with him. Enough said.

- Stay close to your rabbi. He or she can keep you posted about your reputation among executives where it counts, including how they view you, and your performance; not always the same thing. A winning personality can often count as much or more than job performance. Believe it or not, your company's executives are human. Information supplied by your rabbi will alert you to misconceptions that must be changed. Remember, the information that executives receive is filtered through layers of managers. Adversaries within those layers are undoubtedly planting false information about your character and performance. You can't counter vicious lies and innuendo unless you're aware of it.

- Building on the previous point, stay alert to rumors you hear on the grapevine. As we've discussed before, information is king, inside information a kingdom. Don't depend solely on your rabbi. Develop a ring of informants and reward them anytime they feed you valuable information. They'll rally around you if they consider you a winner.

- Remember how I described the need to examine opportunities and pitfalls of any assignment before you undertake it? This is especially important in middle management where most organizational assignments are made. The Boy Scouts said it best: "Be prepared."

- A professional image is crucial. At the lower rungs of the company it may have been okay for you to dress and act informally, but in middle management it's always important to cast an executive image and behave accordingly. Every time an executive comes in contact with you, you're being evaluated. Dress and behave like a drone and you'll be consigned to spend the remainder of your career among drones. Dress and behave like an executive on a mission and you'll enhance your chances of beating an adversary to the next level of the organization.

- Don't hesitate to layoff employees when the orders come down from the top. Dragging your feet while mulling over what functions to cut and which employees to axe will cost you points. Even better, anticipate those orders by laying-off employees before top management issues an edict. Executives reward middle managers with the initiative to reduce headcounts beyond expectations as well as those who understand the importance of keeping costs in line with budget.

- Stay alert to shifts of allegiances in the executive suite. Who's up and who's down is fluid and subject to frequent change. Your rabbi may be in today and out of favor tomorrow. At a moment's notice you may need to develop a new relationship with a top floor executive. Suggestion: Try to develop relationships with more than one executive suite rabbi. Two rabbis are better than one rabbi, and three rabbis are better than two rabbis. You get the picture.

Examples

A middle manager I know named John (not in The Association) fell into the classic trap of finding himself indispensable. He ascended quickly from industrial engineer to second shift production supervisor to department production manager based on his truly fine ability to devise tools and fixtures that cut production delays and increased throughput. It wasn't long before he was promoted to manager of engineering for the entire plant. Under his guidance production flourished and tooling problems, once a mark of the former engineering manager's incompetence, diminished to the point they were no longer major concerns.

John reported to the plant manager for the company's largest plant. His outstanding performance guaranteed him a shot at his boss' job when his boss retired in six months, and he was counting on it. By all rights, the VP of manufacturing should have awarded him the job.

But he didn't. Instead it went to John's peer, the plant's materials manager[28], an adversary of lesser accomplishments than John. John was stunned. He had earned that promotion and he wanted it, was expecting it, and once turned down, he became bitter. John confronted his boss' boss, the vice president of manufacturing, and demanded to know why he hadn't been given the promotion he so rightly deserved (a useless gambit since the decision had already been made). The VP told him that John was greatly respected in the company but so was his peer and it was a toss-up among two highly qualified candidates. He urged John to be patient because the plant manager of the company's second largest manufacturing plant was slotted to become general manager of operations in Taiwan. The VP promised John a shot at the plant manager's job when the move took place. John was not mollified. The company's second largest manufacturing plant was half the size of the one he worked in now.

John persuaded the retiring plant manager to join him for a few celebratory drinks at a local pub in honor of his retirement. Three perfect manhattans loosened the retiree's tongue. He confessed that John was the better qualified candidate but his boss, the vice president of manufacturing, considered John indispensable as head of engineering. He told John that his inability to develop an outstanding replacement all but guaranteed that he would be left behind. Afraid that John's promotion would seriously diminish the plant's engineering capability, or at least seriously impair it, the VP promoted the other guy.

John was yet another victim of linear thinking. He wrongly assumed his technical job skills would earn him a promotion. But technical job skills are seldom enough. As you progress through your corporate career you will find untold numbers of employees whose technical skills earned them promotions from the bottom levels of the organization into middle management. Many then discover, to their dismay, that promotions to the executive suite are based more on contacts and influence and inside information (there's that phrase again) than on technical ability. Indeed, the top is populated with shrewd game players who understand this. The rest are left to drift in middle management.

Here's another example: Andy, an Association management recruit now working for a large national TV studio, told me this story one night at a rare gathering of Association management recruits in a secluded upstate New York mansion:

> "I had it made. At least I thought I had it made. At the time I was a mid-level executive for a TV studio and I was hitting on all eight cylinders. The programs I sponsored were solid hits. I won't identify them because, although we're both in The Association, you know as well as I do we have to keep our mouths shut.[29]
>
> I was in solid with the president of the network and his boss's boss, chairman of the parent company that owned the studio along with prominent newspapers, magazines and financial services firms. I could see beyond the horizon and the picture appeared as rosy as can be. I was riding high and getting cocky and stepped into a trap because of my lack of foresight.
>
> My boss, the network president dropped dead of a heart attack at his desk one sunny Monday morning. I didn't mourn too long because I realized I had been handed a golden opportunity. His job, I believed, was mine.
>
> Murphy's Law rudely intervened and shoved my plans aside. The senior vice president for operations of the parent company was demoted to network president and I was left without any near-term possibility of advancement. That

shook me to the core because I didn't realize he was in such a weak position. All of the companies under his control were performing admirably; sales and profits on target. What I didn't know was that the CEO of the parent company didn't think his senior vice president of operations capable of 'new ideas,' whatever that means. My guess is there was something personal about the senior vice president the CEO didn't like. So, as happens all too frequently in the business world, he demoted the guy.

The only thing that saved my ass was the respect I had garnered for my performance among parent company executives, along with the extensive contacts I cultivated over the years. The CEO took me to lunch and implied that I would soon be promoted. He didn't tell me to what position, but I could guess. Within three months my new boss, the demoted executive, left the company and I was given his job.

I learned a valuable lesson from this experience. It was wrong to assume that just because an executive is meeting his goals he isn't vulnerable. I failed to consider the chairman's personal feelings. That was information I could have uncovered had I kept my ears tuned into executive suite gossip."

Strategies from Section Fourteen

1. Middle management is a jungle that traps the unwary. Only the most observant, the most calculating, the most insightful and the most astute players make it from there to the executive suite. Middle managers take the heat for just about all failures to meet goals, seldom the supervisors who work for them or the executives they work for. The job of middle manager calls for savvy political skills that are often unnecessary at the bottom rungs of the organization, where job performance is king.

2. From a standpoint of sheer numbers, maybe ten percent of all lower level supervisors earn promotions to middle management, and five percent of middle managers (my observation) earn promotions to directors and vice presidents. So the odds are stacked against you for your entire corporate journey. As you ascend the corporate pyramid expect to clash - but never overtly, of course - with increasingly smart and insightful competitors who know those numbers as well as you do now.

3. Minor mistakes your boss excused you for at the lower level of the corporate pyramid when you were young and foolish mushroom into inexcusable errors in middle management where the stakes of the game are proportionately higher. Executives scrutinize middle managers, evaluate their performance more harshly and are less forgiving and tolerant of slips in both performance and political savvy. Middle management, in other words, is that level of the

organization where errors in judgment cost you the most.

4. Middle management is the time to extend your contacts in the executive suite. You're going to get more exposure to the top players. That exposure affords you the opportunity to make more contacts, impress more executives and expand from one to two or more rabbis.

5. If at all possible, get close to a secretary who works for a top executive in your company. These women (you'll find very few male secretaries on the top floor) know everything that's going on, and the lucky guy who gets close to one will receive bountiful tidbits of inside information that may well unlock the door to the executive suite. Maybe some day she'll work for you when you occupy the corner office. As middle manager you'll have more reasons (excuses) to visit the executive suite. Take advantage of it and get yourself a sweetie who can feed you information.

SECTION FIFTEEN

The Management Recruit's Code
of Conduct

Unlike the weasels you will work with in
Corporate America, you must swear to a code
of conduct. Here it is.

Unlike the weasel civilians you work with in Corporate America, you must swear to a code of conduct. Just as a doctor or a cop takes an oath, so must you. But do not confuse your code of conduct with other codes of conduct you hear or read about in the business press. Most of those are phony; window dressing companies promulgate to fool customers, financial analysts and the great American public. Our code of conduct separates you from them. It pertains to your duties and responsibilities to your sponsor, your family and your lifeblood: The Association.

There's a perfectly good reason for a code. As you become more skillful at learning what succeeds and what fails in Corporate America, and as you taste the fruits of your successes, you may be tempted to forget your obligation to The Association. This is not a criticism, nor is it something that happens to all management recruits, just a possibility The Association's psychologists have identified.

Don't forget your roots. The Association placed you in your corporate job and it can take you away from your corporate job. I don't have to elaborate what "take away" means. Don't get so entrenched that you lose perspective.

So, here goes. Your code of conduct in Corporate America:

1. Your first thought in the morning and your last thought at night, and every thought in between, must be about strategies and tactics you need to succeed in Corporate America. That is your obligation both to The Association and to yourself. If your head is screwed on straight, you'll understand they're one and the same.

2. Never consider the feelings of non-Association members in the business world - but be sure to give the appearance of doing so. Remember, they do not belong to the select group you do. They're outsiders, and as such, disposable. Above all, never make any of them close personal friends. (Let me add my two cents: I probably shouldn't have to say this, but I will. Do not drink or take drugs with them.)

3. Hard work is commendable - other people's hard work, because hard work alone does not assure success. The purpose of this career management handbook is to imbue you with that unalterable truth. Pretend to adhere to the Horatio Alger slogans as a cover, provided someone else does the grunt work, takes the fall when necessary to protect you and does not get credit for a successful result. The hard work you do must be directed at climbing the corporate ladder. That is now raison d'être (your purpose in life)[30].

4. Appear to respect your work associates - if they believe you, they're more easily manipulated. However, keep in mind that the higher you go in your company the more likely you are to encounter corporate players who are as vicious as you and less likely to fall for your treacherous schemes. You will have to outthink and outflank them. If your associates and subordinates believe that you are a warm and caring person, your camouflage is compete; they will flock to you. Protective camouflage is important; just make sure it's camouflage only. Warm and caring is incompatible with corporate success.

5. The team approach is crucial; it enables you to blame others for your mistakes.

6. Never step on your corporate associates or friends unless you have to. No reason to be deliberately mean. But when you have to, then be as vicious as need be and keep your dirty schemes sub rosa[31].

7. It's kindly to hold on to failures - they can be controlled and used. Keep one in the wings at all times. You never know when you'll need a fall guy.

8. Sex is not only fun, it's useful, particularly if you get to an executive or an executive secretary. The most successful among you will use your sexual prowess and allure (both male and female management recruits) to seduce several secretaries and executives for fun and profit.

9. Never do anything without a purpose. If you do, at that exact moment you start to drift, and drift is equivalent to failure. You must always be on top of your game.

10. Above all, don't hesitate to do whatever it takes to get ahead.

11. Nothing is out of bounds, provided you don't get caught at it.

END

ENDNOTES

[1] Even here, the wiseguys have wised up. No longer is it an exclusive club for men. That's enough to make the old Sicilian godfathers turn over in their graves.

[2] I would hasten to add that the material they used from my books did not cross the line into illegality or moral turpitude but described what I had found during my career to be useful in climbing the corporate ladder.

[3] Scaring the hell out of me. I had to mentally restrain myself from running off.

[4] A company employee not a member of The Association.

[5] Taxes. You probably never paid any before, but you will now. You cannot afford to be indicted by the government for tax evasion. The Association will provide you with a certified public accountant to do your taxes.

[6] Not his real name, of course.

[7] Both expressed and implied from the text.

[8] You didn't expect me to reveal my real name did you?

[9] Fictitious name, of course.

[10] I'm not exaggerating the numbers. In this era of scarce jobs and countless unemployed and underemployed employees, an ad for a high-paying job with a future, in the newspaper or on the Internet will attract a lot of attention.

[11] The manager of the operation where you will work. For example, sales, finance, or marketing.

[12] Not his real name.

[13] As opposed to an employee, a contractor is not on the company's payroll, but hired for a specific job and then leaves.

[14] CYA = Cover Your Ass

[15] The admonishment to behave toward others as you would have others behave toward you.

[16] Other than The Association, of course. But here I'm referring to the people you work with in Corporate America.

[17] Somebody not a member of The Association.

[18] The steel framework of the car

[19] I changed certain parts of this story in case a snoop from law enforcement should accidentally come across

this information and attempt to trace and identify Miranda.

[20] Ah, a woman who understands the way of the world. How fortunate we are to count her among us.

[21] Miranda was asking the right question. Either breaking into somebody's computer or intercepting e-mail or phone calls is against the law. Violators receive harsh treatment. And the last thing we need is to arouse the interests of law enforcement.

[22] Discussion groups centering about specific subjects. For example, one such group discusses writing novels, another photography.

[23] As usual, a fictitious name.

[24] Shakespeare it isn't, but assembly plant employees know how to express themselves.

[25] Actually, "the price of freedom is eternal vigilance." Whether or not it was Thomas Jefferson who first said it is in contention. Some claim the author as John Philpot Curran. Sometimes the word "liberty" is substituted for "freedom."

[26] I did not mention my home city in this handbook because, should it fall into the wrong hands, that might be enough for savvy law enforcement officers with

sophisticated computer software to narrow down the possibilities of my identity.

[27] Master of Business Administration degree.

[28] The manager responsible for inventory planning and control, production scheduling, purchasing, and shipping and receiving parts and materials.

[29] As you well know management recruits are forbidden to identify themselves to one another. During the occasional times some of us meet we never use names. Failure to comply results in immediate termination from the management program, and you can guess what happens to the silly bastards foolish enough to break silence.

[30] Learn a few French phrases like this. It adds to your camouflage.

[31] Secret. So nobody else recognizes how they're being manipulated.

www.ingramcontent.com/pod-product-compliance
Lightning Source LLC
Chambersburg PA
CBHW021925040426

42448CB00008B/917